the
ultimate
film
guides

A Hard Day's Night

Director
Richard Lester

Note by Lorraine Rolston and Andy Murray

 Longmar

D0256011

Y York Press

York Press
322 Old Brompton Road, London SW5 9JH

Pearson Education Limited
Edinburgh Gate, Harlow, Essex CM20 2JE, United Kingdom
Associated companies, branches and representatives throughout
the world

First published 2001

ISBN 0-582-43245-6

Designed by Vicki Pacey
Phototypeset by Gem Graphics, Trenance, Mawgan Porth, Cornwall
Colour reproduction and film output by Spectrum Colour
Produced by Addison Wesley Longman China Limited, Hong Kong

contents

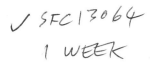

authors of this note Lorraine Rolston has a Masters
degree in Film Studies from Sheffield Hallam University. She is a former
film reviewer for Manchester's City Life magazine. She is currently the
Cinemas Education Officer at Cornerhouse in Manchester.

Andy Murray received a BA in English from Leicester University, and
is currently studying an MA in TV and Radio Scriptwriting at Salford
University. He works at Manchester's Cornerhouse.

background

trailer

a wonderfully lively and altogether good-natured spoof of the juvenile madness called 'Beatlemania'

critic Bosley Crowther

one of the smoothest, freshest, funniest films ever made solely for the purposes of exploitation

Time Magazine

sight gags and documentary realism, semi-abstract, Antonioni-ish chases, a Fellini helicopter ... All contribute to making *A Hard Day's Night* a truly fresh, lively length of film

Newsweek

after that movie was released everyone knew the names of all four Beatles ... everyone

critic Roger Ebert

the Citizen Kane of juke box movies

film historian Andrew Sarris

I want a film that can stand on its own without the Beatles

screenwriter Alun Owen

what could have been simply a money-making gimmick turns out as nimble entertainment in its own right. It's offbeat – and on the beat. It's a winner

critic Dick Richards, Daily Mirror

works on a level at which most British films ... don't manage to get going at all

Sight and Sound

We all quite liked it. There were only one or two moments when we didn't

Beatle Paul McCartney

reading a hard day's night

It's doubtful anyone involved in the making of *A Hard Day's Night* would have expected, at the time, that the film would merit critical attention nearly forty years later. When released by United Artists in July 1964, it was intended as a cheap and quickly executed **exploitation picture**, aimed at the youth market, to cash in on the burgeoning success of four young Liverpudlian musicians called the Beatles. Initially the film was, for United Artists, simply a by-product of a deal to release a lucrative soundtrack album. Cynical observers of the day predicted that the Beatles' phenomenon wouldn't last. Nevertheless, to their great credit, all concerned in the making of the film endeavoured to create something a cut above the uninspired pop-star music vehicles that proceeded it. As a result, the film didn't so much rewire the **genre** as throw it away and start afresh. What began as a cheap exploitation project has now become a pop culture artefact.

A Hard Day's Night captures a crucial moment in postwar popular culture. The 'baby boom' generation was moving into adulthood, and redefining social mores. The film skilfully makes reference to the key themes of the time – the generation gap, class differences, the new phenomenon of pop celebrity – whilst remaining imaginative and entertaining and, crucially, communicating through cinema the thrill of the Beatles' music and performance.

The **story** of *A Hard Day's Night* is that of a collaboration: between its **director** Richard Lester, then in the early stages of a fascinating, creative film career; and the Beatles, the phenomenally successful pop stars – still on the ascendant to world stardom – who agreed to star in, and compose fresh songs for, the movie that would break them into the film business.

the most important group in pop music history

the beatles: a brief history

At the dawn of the twenty-first century, the Beatles have sold over an estimated one billion records and are indisputably the single most important group in pop music history. But when *A Hard Day's Night* came to be made in early 1964, their career was still in its early stages and their reputation was less unshakeable.

The band had formed around a nucleus of bass guitarist Paul McCartney and guitarist John Lennon. The two had met as teenage schoolboys at St Peter's Parish Church fete in July 1957 and had bonded over their mutual love of early American rock 'n' roll by the likes of Elvis Presley and Carl Perkins. McCartney joined Lennon's skiffle group the Quarrymen, soon bringing in his friend, 14-year-old local guitarist George Harrison. They were in turn supplemented by drummer Pete Best and Lennon's art-school friend Stuart Sutcliffe on bass.

Allan Williams, a local promoter, began to find work for the ambitious group. Discovering a demand for English beat groups in Hamburg, Williams shipped his charges – now renamed the Silver Beatles – to play a residency in the Hamburg Kaiserkeller in late 1960. During their time in this rough-and-ready atmosphere, the band honed their abilities as musicians, building up a vast repertoire of cover versions and learning to entertain often hostile and unsympathetic audiences. Return engagements to Hamburg followed over the next two years – although Stu Sutcliffe elected to leave the band and stay there with his girlfriend, Astrid. Tragically, he died soon after.

The band's name had now become simply the Beatles, and back in Liverpool their reputation was burgeoning. They began to write their own songs and took up a residency at The Cavern, a local club, from where their fame spread. Local Jewish businessman Brian Epstein became aware of the band's popularity after repeated requests for records by them were made at his record shop. Epstein duly sought the band out, and was impressed enough to offer them a management contract. Despite having no previous pop management experience, Epstein weathered a lack of interest from the majority of British record companies to eventually sign the Beatles to EMI Records in October 1962. A result of the signing was that Pete Best, whose drumming was considered substandard, was sacked from the group. He was replaced by Richard Starkey – aka Ringo Starr – a long-time fixture of the Liverpool music scene, whom the Beatles had met in Hamburg.

The Beatles achieved national chart success with their early singles 'Please Please Me', 'She Loves You' and 'Love Me Do'. By 1964, they had released three hit albums and the international best-selling single 'I Wanna Hold Your Hand'. The band toured worldwide; a massive promotional campaign laid the foundations for their arrival in America; in February 1964, they appeared on the popular Ed Sullivan show, to record-breaking audiences of 70 million viewers. The band were now international superstars.

When United Artists embarked on a plan to make a feature film starring the band in the Spring of 1964, it was essential that the film be made and released as quickly as possible. It was assumed that the Beatles' moment of fame would be brief.

key players' biographies

JOHN LENNON (HIMSELF)

Born in Liverpool on 9 October 1940 during a Luftwaffe air raid, Lennon was a teenage fan of rock 'n' roll and skiffle music, even forming his own band, the Quarrymen. In due course, schoolmate Paul McCartney joined the band, which developed into the Beatles.

Aged seventeen, Lennon's mother was killed in a road accident. His father had disappeared when he was two and Lennon mostly grew up living with his mother's sister Mimi. In time, his band the Beatles were signed to EMI and Lennon's songwriting partnership with Paul McCartney yielded worldwide hit singles. Lennon's life-long love of wordplay and drawing led to the publication of two poetry books at the height of the band's fame: *In His Own Write* (1964) and *A Spaniard in The Works* (1965).

Lennon found it difficult to show deference to a film director

Both were well received, garnering Lennon serious literary success.

Lennon's film career subsequent to *A Hard Day's Night* was checkered. He was dismissive of *Help!* (1965) and showed little interest in *Magical Mystery Tour* (1967) or *Yellow Submarine* (1968). His appearance in *Let It Be* (1970) is remarkable only for his almost catatonic appearance and irregular verbal interjections. His interest was focused upon his lover, Yoko Ono, a Japanese avant-garde artist. Together they created experimental soundscapes and in time their own underground films, amongst them *Two Virgins*, *Self-portrait* and *Fly*.

Always a powerful personality, Lennon found it difficult to suppress himself and show deference to a film director. His performance in *A Hard Day's Night*, whilst perfectly engaging, was nevertheless judged by critics to be inferior to the natural ease of Ringo Starr. His independent acting career never took off. When the Beatles abandoned live performances in 1966, Lennon jetted off immediately to Spain to film his role in Richard Lester's *How I Won The War*. The antiwar tone of the film didn't win it many fans, with many World War veterans still alive: and although Lennon's large role as Sergeant Gripweed was a respected performance, further roles failed to appear. Richard Lester even displayed some regret at casting the Beatle in a non-Beatle role: 'I'm sorry in a way that John Lennon was in the film because it creates an imbalance. The part just seemed to fit John, though I didn't want to make a film with a Beatle in it.'

Lennon continued his musical career, becoming increasingly experimental with sound and words through such classic Beatles projects as *Sergeant Pepper's Lonely Hearts Club Band* (1967) and *Magical Mystery Tour* (1967). The surreal word-play in evidence in his books was used to fine effect in later Beatles lyrics, notably 'I Am the Walrus' and 'Across the Universe'. Following the Beatles split, he started strongly with a solo career that began with the stark, confessional album *Plastic Ono Band* (1970). His output waned into the mid-1970s, as he became a 'house husband' to his wife Yoko and son Sean, and notoriously mastered the art of baking bread. He was attempting a musical comeback with the *Double Fantasy* album (1980), when a psychotic fan, Mark Chapman,

biographies background

assassinated him outside his family home in the Dakota Building, New York, on December 9 1980.

PAUL MCCARTNEY (HIMSELF)

Born James Paul McCartney in Liverpool on 18 June 1942, McCartney came from musical stock. His father, a cotton salesman, moonlighted in a popular local jazz band. The young Paul was fascinated by the new wave of American rock 'n' rollers, and his parents gave in to requests to buy their young son a guitar. In time, he befriended an older schoolmate, John Lennon, and joined his band. Within five years the band had become the Beatles, and released their first hit single.

McCartney showed a keen interest in the film world, not least by his engagement in 1966 to popular film actress Jane Asher. He met controversial playwright Joe Orton to commission the writing of *Up Against It*, a screenplay for a proposed third Beatles / United Artists film. Upon the death of Beatles manager Brian Epstein, McCartney stepped up his involvement within the band, acting as the *de facto* leader. He instigated the *Magical Mystery Tour* (1967) project and is credited as the chief 'director' of the resulting film. He wrote the score for *The Family Way* (1966) without the other Beatles, and can be seen in the documentary *Let It Be* (1970) to be effectively commanding his fellow band members – often to their great chagrin.

McCartney's involvement with the film world continued slowly but steadily, although chiefly in the capacity of musician. With his 1970's band Wings, he wrote and recorded the theme to the James Bond film *Live and Let Die* (1973), even insisting upon providing the vocals himself although the film's producers requested a female singer.

A flurry of work followed in the 1980s: the theme to the espionage comedy *Spies Like Us* (1985) and his own poorly received feature, *Give My Regards To Broad Street* (1984), in which he appeared as himself alongside his wife Linda and Ringo Starr. With a keen interest in popular culture – not to mention the finances accrued from an incomparably successful songwriting career – McCartney bought the film rights to the Daily Express children's strip *Rupert the Bear*. His 1986 hit *We All Stand*

Together – credited to 'Rupert and the Frog Chorus', and furnished with a fully animated music video – was to be the springboard for a full animated musical feature. Despite the success of the single, the film failed to materialise.

Following the release in the 1990s of *The Beatles Anthology* – a series of televised documentaries and three record sets of unreleased Beatles material – McCartney continues to record music and received considerable acclaim for his 1998 album *Flaming Pie* – which some observers claimed represented a return to his songwriting style from the Beatles days.

GEORGE HARRISON (HIMSELF)

Born in Wavertree, Liverpool on 25 February 1943, Harrison was only fourteen when he joined the band that eventually became the Beatles. His role as the band's junior member came to irk him, particularly as his band mates Lennon and McCartney were lauded songwriters, and Harrison's own songs only rarely appeared on Beatles' albums. On leaving the band, he recorded a vast backlog of songs as *All Things Must Pass* (1970), a three-album set, to great acclaim.

Although Harrison's performance in *A Hard Day's Night* was perfectly satisfactory, he never took an acting role outside of a Beatles film. Indeed, his role in *Magical Mystery Tour* (1967) is virtually silent. Nevertheless, he maintained involvement in the film industry which came to surpass all his fellow ex-Beatles. Harrison's first solo excursion into film came in 1968, when he recorded the score for *Wonderwall*. The instrumental soundtrack album, made in Bombay using thirteen Indian musicians, counts as the first solo work by any Beatle.

In 1972 he was heavily involved in The Concert for Bangladesh, a fundraising initiative to provide financial help for the inhabitants of the flood-struck country. He was producer of the best-selling soundtrack album, and a film of the concert was released.

In 1979 Harrison was approached by the Monty Python comedy team: they were about to begin production of their film *Life Of Brian*, when finances from EMI fell through due to hesitancy about the controversial religious content. Having obtained funding for their previous film *Monty Python and the Holy Grail* (1975) from wealthy rock stars – including Led Zeppelin and Pink Floyd – the team thought Harrison might be willing to make an investment. In fact, Harrison went so far as to form a film company – Handmade Films – with his business partner Dennis O'Dell. (Harrison was also sufficiently good-humoured to take a cameo role in Monty Python member Eric Idle's Beatles spoof, *The Rutles: All You Need Is Cash* (1978).)

Monty Python's *Life of Brian* was a huge success, and Handmade went on to fund an impressive series of films throughout the 1980s, effectively becoming Britain's foremost film company of the period. Handmade's successes included *The Long Good Friday* (1980), *Time Bandits* (1981) – for which Harrison provided the closing song – *A Private Function* (1984), *Mona Lisa* (1986), and *Withnail and I* (1987) which cheekily features Harrison's Beatles song *While My Guitar Gently Weeps*. Handmade went bankrupt in the 1990s, prompting Harrison's somewhat uneasy participation in the reunited Beatles *Anthology* project, allegedly for financial reasons.

RINGO STARR (HIMSELF)

Born Richard Starkey in 7 July 1940, the eldest Beatle was rechristened 'Ringo' by his band mates in Rory Storm's Hurricanes, due to his penchant for wearing finger jewellery. Having been a regular on the Liverpool music scene, and having met the band in Hamburg, Ringo was an obvious choice as the Beatles' replacement drummer when the band sacked Pete Best.

Starr's performance in *A Hard Day's Night* was much lauded, leading many to believe that he of all the Beatles had natural acting ability. Starr himself makes light of this, explaining that his spotlight scenes in the film, wandering through London and befriending a boy, were only so natural because he was drunk during filming. Nevertheless, the acclaim was a godsend to Starr, whose role in the Beatles was restricted to drumming – with a rare vocal and even rarer songwriting credit. He was awarded a crucial role in the planned second Beatles film: his part in

Help! (1965) is substantial. Even so, a full acting career eluded him. He took roles in *Candy* (1968), *The Magic Christian* (1969), Frank Zappa's *200 Motels* (1971), *That'll Be the Day* (1973) and *Caveman* (1981). Starr became friendly with ex-Goon Peter Sellers, who introduced him to the novels of Terry Southern, from which both *Candy* and *The Magic Christian* were adapted.

As a solo artist, Starr famously became the first Beatle to achieve a Number One single. Despite continued support in his musical endeavours from his fellow ex-Beatles, this promising start petered out through the 1970s. Starr tried his hand at directing with *Born to Boogie* (1972) appeared in Paul McCartney's poorly received *Give My Regards to Broad Street* (1984). His chief claim to fame in recent years has been as the lugubrious narrator of the children's television series *Thomas the Tank Engine and Friends*. However, he didn't contribute to Thomas's film debut, *Thomas and the Haunted Railroad* (2000).

RICHARD LESTER (DIRECTOR)

Born in Philadelphia, USA, in January 1932, Lester's early days clearly signposted his precocious talent. He could read at the age of three, and could write music by the age of twelve. He himself has jokingly claimed, 'My mother fed me a bit of royal jelly'. At the age of fifteen, he began a university degree in clinical psychology. On graduation he took a somewhat sideways step – to become a staff director for his local television station, WCAU. This proved to be a rich training ground for Lester, but not a full career: 'I felt that there was a great possibility that I would be a has-been at twenty-two; so I thought ... I'd escape and see whether the rest of the world existed'. Lester found himself travelling through Europe finding work as a journalist and jazz pianist before arriving in London in the mid-1950s.

He was quickly employed to share directing chores on the television serial *Mark Sabre* (during 1956–7) with future luminary Joseph Losey, who would go on to direct *The Loneliness of the Long Distance Runner* (1962) and *The Servant* (1963). Lester soon found himself in the company of the Goons – the seminal, surreal radio comedy team, then attempting to move into television and film. Lester found he could appreciate this seemingly exclusively British sense of humour. 'Whenever people said, "how can an American deal with English comedy?" I said "it's the same – we're laughing at the same things".

Undoubtedly the pivotal point in Lester's career came on two consecutive Sunday afternoons in 1959. With the intention of making essentially a home movie, Lester was placed in charge of Goon comedian Peter Sellers's latest film equipment – a professional-standard 16mm camera. Also utilising the comic talents of Spike Milligan, Graham Stark and Mario Fabrizi, the resulting eleven minutes of footage was put together as the bizarre, silent short *The Running, Jumping Standing Still Film*. Although never made for anything other than the private amusement of the participants (at a total cost of £70), word spread on the grapevine that the piece deserved a wider audience. In due course, it was screened at the Edinburgh Festival and later the San Francisco Festival, and was even nominated for an Academy Award. On the finished article, Lester was credited as actor, writer, director, cinematographer and composer.

Lester's subsequent attempts to start a film-directing career stalled. Lester says now, 'Everyone loved [*The Running, Jumping Standing Still Film*], and said, if we ever want a ninety minute version, we'll let you know. But they never did'. Lester found gainful employment directing television commercials, which allowed him to experiment stylistically with cutting and editing. He still hoped to get into cinema, and a break came when writer/director Milton Subotsky required a director for his quickly-made exploitation feature *It's Trad Dad!* (1961), featuring a linked stream of appearances from pop stars of the day such as John Leyton and The Temperance Seven. Lester imbued this, his feature film debut, with commendable energy and visual flair. In 1959, American expatriate film producer Walter Shenson had made a great success of the Peter Sellers comedy vehicle *The Mouse That Roared*. The 1963 sequel, *Mouse on the Moon*, provided Lester with his second film-directing job. Although neither a smash hit nor an extraordinary piece of film making, it was vital in building a relationship between producer Shenson and his director. When Shenson was co-opted into producing a film starring the latest

Lester's surreal, comic-book leanings

Liverpudlian pop sensations soon after, he immediately approached Lester to direct. Lester managed to use the quickly made pop-star movie as a vehicle for his interests in *cinéma vérité*, documentary realism, surreal visual comedy and music-related imagery (see Style).

The massive impact of *A Hard Day's Night* guaranteed Lester further film work. In 1965 he made *The Knack ... and How To Get It,* a stylish examination of Swinging Sixties morality. The same year, Lester returned to direct the Beatles second film, *Help!* (1965). Although the Beatles themselves were wary of the change in tone of this follow-up – famously remarking that they felt 'like extras in our own film' – *Help!* was another big success. With its strong visual style and zany humour, *Help!* perhaps reflects Lester's own surreal, comic-book leanings more than *A Hard Day's Night* had done.

Throughout the 1960s, Lester directed a number of striking films which did much to examine the mood and nature of the decade. Even his adaptation of the stage success *A Funny Thing Happened on the Way to the Forum* (1966), set in Ancient Rome, reflects as much on sixties attitudes as on those of the setting. Lester's antiwar satire *How I Won The War* (1967), this time an adaptation of a novel by Patrick Ryan, stirred up much controversy. Lester's next film *Petulia* (1968) starred perennial sixties icon Julie Christie, and again examined the mores of the times, although Lester's style appeared to be maturing, and growing less frantic and zany. His planned follow-up was to have been outrageous playwright Joe Orton's *Up Against It* – a script written for, but rejected by, the Beatles. (At the time the search was still on for the prospective third Beatles film: Lester was not involved, and had evidently sought to make a career on being more than simply 'the Beatles man'.) Lester filmed former Goon Spike Milligan's surreal post-apocalyptic stage play *The Bed-Sitting Room* (1969). Featuring comedy actor Arthur Lowe alongside comedy double act Peter Cook and Dudley Moore, *The Bed-Sitting Room* follows the struggles of a group of humans after a nuclear war, as they gradually metamorphose into items of furniture as a result of fallout. As a return to Lester's anarchic comedy roots, the film failed to draw audiences and Lester's career fell into a fallow period.

Owen had a reputation for being adaptable

Lester's later films often focus on the adventures of folk heroes. His version of Alexandra Dumas's French swashbuckling *The Three Musketeers* (1973) was a major hit, immediately spawning a sequel – *The Four Musketeers* (1974). (Ironically, *The Three Musketeers* had earlier been earmarked as a potential Beatles film, although Lester wasn't attached to the project.) More modern folk heroes were the subjects of *Butch and Sundance: The Early Years* (1979). Lester also made a number of more thoughtful films such as *Juggernaut* (1974), a satire on the then-current disaster movie boom; and *Robin and Marian* (1976). Lester's last major project was as director of both *Superman II* (1980) and *Superman III* (1983). Both were major international hits.

In 1991, Lester renewed his Beatles associations by directing *Get Back*, a feature film documenting a live concert appearance by Paul McCartney.

ALUN OWEN (SCRIPTWRITER)

Alun Owen was born in Menai Bridge in November 1925. Perhaps surprisingly, the man chosen to write the dialogue for *A Hard Day's Night*'s young Liverpudlian stars was a 39-year-old Welshman. However, Owen had a reputation for being adaptable, to put it mildly.

His early life in North Wales included a two-year stint working down coalmines as part of a World War Two initiative. An interest in theatre saw him join the Perth repertory company as an assistant stage manager. Although Welsh was Owen's first language, it was necessary to adapt to English when his family moved to Liverpool.

After a stab at acting, Owen eventually found his true calling as a writer. His first play, *Progress in the Park*, began life in 1959 as a BBC Radio production before transferring to the stage. This was followed by *The Rough and Ready Lot*, concerning British mercenaries hiding in South America in the mid nineteenth century. A flurry of writing work in 1960 included his first feature film, *The Criminal*, a prison drama starring Stanley Baker as a gangster finishing a fifteen-year sentence and going in search of his hidden loot. The film's director was Joseph Losey, a former television colleague of Richard Lester.

a bit phoney

Perhaps Owen's finest hour was as a television dramatist: he was the writer of acclaimed works such as *After the Funeral* (1960) and *Lena, O My Lena* (1960), and most importantly *The Strain* and *No Trams on Lime Street* (1959). The latter pieces explicitly documented modern life in Owen's adopted home of Liverpool. It was this, along with his previous work with Richard Lester, that made Owen such an ideal candidate to write the Beatles' first film. When first choice Johnny Speight turned the job down, Owen was engaged to work on the script – after first meeting the band to gain some insight into their individual characters. The end result was received to mixed responses from the band. (George Harrison, in particular, took exception to the term 'grotty' which he was required to say in the film. Harrison has claimed that Owen made the word up.) 'It was a good projection of one facade of us, which was on tour' explains McCartney. Lennon was less diplomatic. 'Alun Owen was a bit phoney ... He stayed with us for two days and wrote the whole thing based on our characters then: mine – witty; Ringo – dumb and cute; George this, Paul that.' (Legend has it that Lennon took exception to Welsh-born Owen's attempts to act as a Scouser, accusing the writer of being 'nothing but an amateur Liverpudlian'. Owen retorted that this was preferable to being a professional Liverpudlian.)

Oddly, at this very point when Owen's career seemed so full of promise, it evaporated. He never wrote another produced screenplay, nor television play, nor indeed worked again as an actor. Owen nevertheless remained happy to discuss his part in the story of *A Hard Day's Night*, and appeared in a twentieth anniversary television special *Making of A Hard Day's Night* – alongside many other original participants in the project. Alun Owen died in London in December 1994, aged 69.

WILFRED BRAMBELL (PAUL'S GRANDFATHER)

Born in Dublin in 1912, Wilfred Brambell joined the local Abbey Theatre in his youth, and went on to make several appearances on the London stage during the 1930s. Brambell's first television appearances were all small roles in works by legendary television writer Nigel Kneale: *The Quatermass Experiment* (1953), a haunting adaptation of *1984* (1954),

'You dirty old man!'

and *Quatermass II* (1955). He became a successful character actor for film and television; notable roles include that of the Postman in Loch Ness Monster comedy *What a Whopper!* (1961) and as Bill Gaye in Disney's *In Search of The Castaways* (1962). To contemporary British viewers of *A Hard Day's Night*, though, Brambell was familiar for one particular role – that of old Albert Steptoe in the BBC comedy series *Steptoe and Son*. The series began in 1962 as 'The Offer', a one-off entry into Comedy Playhouse, a showcase for writers Ray Galton and Alan Simpson. Due to an encouraging public response, a full series was commissioned, eventually running until 1974. As Albert Steptoe, Brambell would be seen harassing Harry H. Corbett as his son Harold, his partner in an East End rag and bone business. Albert Steptoe's unhygienic demeanour was the root of Harold's disgusted catch phrase 'You dirty old man!'. (This in turn leads to a running joke in *A Hard Day's Night* where Brambell, as Paul's Grandfather, is repeatedly declared to be 'very clean'.)

Brambell was 52 years old at the time *A Hard Day's Night* was made. Other roles followed in *Carry On Again, Doctor* (1969) – an entry into the long-running *Carry On* series – and a brief cameo in the acclaimed *Witchfinder General* (1968). A feature version of *Steptoe and Son* appeared in 1972, and a sequel, *Steptoe and Son Ride Again*, in 1973. Sadly, Brambell's film career arguably started too late in life. With few major film credits to his name, Brambell died of cancer in January 1985, aged seventy-two.

NORMAN ROSSINGTON (NORM)

Norman Rossington was himself a natural Liverpudlian, born on Christmas Eve, 1928. He worked as a carpenter and a messenger boy down at the Liverpool docks before studying to be a draughtsman. He was sidetracked by joining a local drama group at the age of nineteen, and he subsequently moved to Bristol, and then to London, for the sake of his nascent acting career. During lean times, he worked as a chef in police canteens.

Rossington first made his name as an actor as Private Cupcake in the ITV sitcom *The Army Game* in the late 1950s, which led in turn to film roles including that of Herbert Brown in an army-based British comedy entitled *Carry On Sergeant* (1958). The film spawned the legendary *Carry On* series, and Rossington also appeared in *Carry On Nurse* (1958), as well as in *Carry On Regardless* (1961). By the early 1960s Rossington was becoming a familiar face to British audiences (a face, in fact, which he himself described as 'a mug like a jug'). He was Bert in the seminal *Saturday Night and Sunday Morning* (1960), a key film in the 'British New Wave' (see Style: Location). Roles followed as Private Clough in *The Longest Day* (1962), Corporal Jenkis in David Lean's *Lawrence of Arabia* (1962) and, of course, as Norm in *A Hard Day's Night*. Across the Atlantic, he took the role of Arthur Babcock in another pop-star vehicle – Elvis Presley's *Double Trouble* (1967). A career high, and his own personal favourite role, came as Corbett in *The Charge of The Light Brigade* (1965).

Whilst never becoming a big box-office name, Rossington worked continuously in film and television for the next thirty years – notably starring as Sergeant Rogers in cult British horror film *Deathline* (1972) and as Tom in *Digby, The Biggest Dog in the World* (alongside Victor Spinetti, 1973). In the same year, he played an impassioned Liverpool docker in playwright Jim Allen's television piece *The Big Flame* (1969).

Rossington continued to work enthusiastically in theatre for the rest of his career, not least as part of The Royal Shakespeare Company. He worked extensively in musicals, setting a record with 567 consecutive performances of *Guys and Dolls* – only to break the record himself with performances of *Beauty and the Beast*. During the 1990s, he took small roles in British films *The Krays* (1990) and *Let Him Have it* (1991), and appeared in the high-budget ITV drama *Sharpe's Regiment* (1996). He died, aged seventy, in May 1999.

VICTOR SPINETTI (TV DIRECTOR)

Despite his appearance in *A Hard Day's Night* as a nerve-shredded television director, the real-life Victor Spinetti is first and foremost a theatre man. Born to an Italian father and a Welsh mother, the young Spinetti attended the College of Music and Drama in Cardiff. He quickly made a name for himself as a sure-footed comic actor, winning a Tony

it was as if we'd known each other all our lives

Award for his role as The Drill Sergeant Major in the stage play *Oh What a Lovely War!* in 1964. In the same year, he made an impression on cinema-goers in *A Hard Day's Night*.

Film roles followed in adaptations of plays such as *The Taming of the Shrew* (1967) and Dylan Thomas's *Under Milk Wood* (1971). Having become firm friends with the Beatles – 'When we met it was as if we'd known each other all our lives ... I just loved them' (Neaverson, 1997, p. 20) – Spinetti made appearances in both of the band's subsequent live-action adventures, as Doctor Foot in *Help!* (1965) and as an Army Recruitment Sergeant in *Magical Mystery Tour* (1967) (see Contexts: The Beatles' Film Career). He also adapted and directed John Lennon's poetry book *In His Own Write* for the stage in 1969.

Spinetti renewed his pop-star associations by appearing in *Under The Cherry Moon* (1986), starring and directed by the multitalented Eighties icon Prince. Spinetti's career continues to this day, talking in cartoon voiceovers (British television series Superted), and his first love, theatre.

JOHN JUNKIN (SHAKE)

Despite appearing in *A Hard Day's Night* as a Liverpudlian friend of the Beatles, John Junkin was in fact born in Ealing, London, in January 1930. A well-loved British character actor with a penchant for comedy, Junkin has appeared in a vast variety of television parts, including roles in *Coronation Street*, *Z-Cars* and *All Creatures Great and Small*. Film work has included *The Wrong Box* (1966) and Richard Lester's *How I Won The War* (1967).

In recent times Junkin has been a programme associate and writer for, amongst others, the BBC's *Noel's House Party*. He continues to work on British television, and has appeared in high-profile 1990s series such as *The Bill*, *Mr Bean* and *Inspector Morse*.

'We waited until something far better turned up'

making a hard day's night

The reason for making *A Hard Day's Night* was never in doubt. The film's first working title was simply *Beatles*. The whole exercise was intended just to get the band up on the screen where their adoring fans could pay to see them in close-up.

The film's origin as an exploitation picture goes even deeper than that. In the first instance United Artists decided to make it simply as a means of releasing an album of original Beatles' songs. The film's attendant lucrative soundtrack album was therefore the lure for United Artists.

The Beatles were certainly looking to move into the movies. One early offer was to appear in *The Yellow Teddybears*, about a group of young tearaway girls from Peterbridge Grammar School. The Beatles' planned appearance would have been in scenes set in the excitement of London – but when it became clear that the band might be performing songs written by other hands, or even give up copyright to new compositions of their own, any enthusiasm faded. Paul McCartney explained later, 'We turned that offer down and waited until something far better turned up' (Carr, 1996, p. 12).

United Artists forged a deal with Beatles manager Brian Epstein via George Ornstein, the company's head of European production. Initially Epstein settled for 7.5% of the net profits from the venture, plus £20,000 cash. This was agreed without the necessary say-so from the film company's chiefs. The project was nevertheless green-lighted by Ornstein's superiors, purely because the costs were so cheap. In fact, Ornstein renegotiated with Epstein, raising the Beatles' share of profits to £25,000 plus 20% of profits. This increase was not merely a gesture of goodwill: Ornstein wished to fully secure the services of the Beatles whose worldwide popularity was increasing quickly. An additional clause entitled United Artists to make a total of three films starring the Beatles, with incrementally increasing profits for the band.

'The Beatles? Who are they?'

Ornstein swiftly installed Walter Shenson as producer of the project. Previously, Shenson has produced the British comedies *The Mouse That Roared* (1959) and its sequel, *Mouse on the Moon* (1963). Initially, Shenson's response to this new project was a discouraging 'The Beatles? Who are they?' But once becoming involved in the life of the band, Shenson summoned up enthusiasm for the film and conceived a basic 'day in the life' format for it; as he witnessed, a day in the life of the Beatles was extraordinary. 'Every time the cab stopped in traffic, one or more of them would dash out and buy a newspaper, [and] open it to see if they were featured in it' (Walker, 1974, p. 234).

Perhaps surprisingly for an exploitation picture, and to the credit of Walter Shenson, serious thought was given as to who should write and direct the embryonic Beatles film. At first, front runner to write the script was left-wing comedy scriptwriter Johnny Speight. At the time Speight was responsible for '*Til Death Us Do Part*, the sitcom vehicle for the inimitable Alf Garnett character. Garnett, a working-class Jew, weekly regaled his family – and hence the viewing nation – with his laughably ill-informed prejudices. Memorably, he would dismiss his Liverpudlian son-in-law as a 'randy scouse git' – which might have attracted the attention of the world's most famous scousers. Nevertheless, writer Speight declined the offer to write their movie.

Instead, the job fell to Alun Owen. But the film still needed a director. In retrospect, the choice of Richard Lester seems almost predestined. Lester was an American expatriate, perfectly complementing the Beatles' own adoration of American pop culture. Lester had previously worked with the Goons, a seminal, surreal comedy team led by Spike Milligan. The Beatles were firm fans of the Goons, and their record producer George Martin also had experience of working with the team on their commercial recordings. (Notably, Richard Lester had also worked with the Goons on an assortment of film and television projects, and had directed for the Goon-related television show Son of Fred, also featuring Alun Owen.)

Lester had a wealth of experience of directing television, and had recently made two key entries into film directing that made him perfect

'Oh, What a Lovely Wart!'

for the Beatles job. Firstly, he had directed *The Running, Jumping Standing Still Film* (1959). The Beatles all knew of and loved the short film, and its influence is certainly felt in *A Hard Day's Night*, most obviously in the outdoor 'Can't Buy Me Love' sequence. (see Style).

Lester's second key credit came as director of *It's Trad Dad!* (1961). The film takes the form of a music documentary, detailing the craze for 'trad jazz'. Lester creates a warm, energetic piece that communicates the joys of that particular period in modern music. As such, he became the natural choice to capture the manic thrills of the Beatles and their music on celluloid.

With the key personnel in place, work on the film could begin in earnest. Lester and Owen were despatched to meet the Beatles in Paris in January 1964, and subsequently spent several days in their company in order to garner an insight into their personalities, and hence 'research' the characters for the script.

The Beatles returned from a triumphant first visit to America to begin writing and recording songs for the film's soundtrack in late February 1964. On 2 March they presented Richard Lester with tapes of nine songs for potential inclusion in the finished film, from which Lester chose seven – 'Can't Buy Me Love', 'I Should Have Known Better', 'If I Fell', 'I'm Happy Just to Dance With You', 'And I Love Her', 'Tell Me Why' and 'You Can't Do That'. That same day, filming began of the crowds of screaming fans at Paddington Station, and the making of the film was underway. One problem remained. The film still had no official title. It was being unofficially referred to as the *Beatles* or *Beatles Movie*, and was for a while going to be called Beatlemania. But it was hoped that one of the new songs written for the film might have a title that would lend itself to the whole enterprise. In the event, that didn't happen. For one thing, most of the songs had overt 'love song' titles, and there was no romance in the film. The band continued to make suggestions for titles of varied usefulness – including John Lennon's favourite, 'Oh, What a Lovely Wart!'. Inspiration finally came when least expected. After a heavy day of work in the studio, Ringo was heard to declare that it wasn't so much a hard day; due to the late hour, it was more rightly 'a hard day's night'. John

making background

Lennon passed the magic phrase on to producer Walter Shenson, who delightedly re-christened the film and despatched McCartney and Lennon to write a title song around it (see Soundtrack).

Filming for *A Hard Day's Night* started on 2 March 1964 and finished less than eight weeks later, on 24 April. Problems slowing the hectic schedule down were mainly caused by the band's eager fans. In particular, it was feared that information was being leaked by a member of the production team, tipping-off fans as to the outdoor filming locations. Eventually, filming for the opening railway sequence moved from Paddington to Marylebone Station, taking place on two consecutive Sunday mornings in April. Time was lost in attempting a stop-motion effect dance sequence, featuring the Lionel Blair dancers, intended to accompany 'You Can't Do That'. The results were unsatisfactory and so the half-a-day's footage proved unusable. Lester nevertheless proved highly adaptable to the chaos surrounding the Beatles. On 23 April, group scenes of the band were successfully shot – with some careful photography – despite the absence of John Lennon, who was elsewhere promoting his book *In His Own Write*.

In all, the eight-week period seemed to the Beatles to drag a little. Says Paul McCartney, 'We didn't know how long it took to make a movie … We could have done a couple of tours, written a few new songs and cut an album … but to the people working on the film set, eight weeks was a comparatively short time'. (Carr, 1996, p. 24). Famously, the film-makers faced pressure from their American superiors to dub the Beatles' accents in post-production to make them clearer for international audiences; but the makers held firm. 'If we can understand a cowboy talkin' Texan,' argued McCartney, 'they can understand us talkin' Liverpool'.

Due to the soundtrack deal that had brought *A Hard Day's Night* into being in the first case, the film was put in a unique position. Advanced sales of the soundtrack album were so huge that the film was in fact in profit before it was even released. The soundtrack became the biggest-selling album of all time (up to that point) and an ecstatic United Artists announced that the film would be playing on a saturation basis all over the globe by September 1964, with 'more prints in circulation that any other pic in history'. In America, the film's profits after six weeks were approaching $6 million. Worldwide, the film's takings eventually topped $11 million.

A Hard Day's Night was released on 6 July in the UK, and 12 August in America. The British premiere took place at the British Pavilion in London's Piccadilly Circus. Over 20,000 fans arrived to greet the debuting actors-cum-musicians. Royalty was present, too, in the form of Princess Margaret. On meeting the Princess, McCartney humbly declared, 'I don't think we are very good, ma'am, but we had a very good producer and director' (Carr, 1996, p. 29).

director as auteur

Developed by French film critics in the 1960s, the 'auteur' theory suggests that, despite the large number of people at work on a film, ultimately one individual is responsible for the vision within the finished article. This 'auteur' (literally 'author') is usually – but not always – the director. A director's status as auteur can be ascertained by studying other films by the same film maker. A visionary 'auteur' director's films will share themes, approaches and preoccupations.

It may seem unusual to consider Richard Lester as an auteur. At the point in his career when *A Hard Day's Night* was made, he was a relatively new director, with a background in television and commercials. The film itself was purely an exploitative star vehicle. The only guiding hand behind it might reasonably be presumed to be market forces. Nevertheless, *A Hard Day's Night* does display many of the significant hallmarks which, in retrospect, are present throughout all of Richard Lester's films.

Music is a common motif. As Lester himself is a keen musician (and indeed provides the score for *The Running, Jumping Standing Still Film,* 1959) it's understandable that this interest should be reflected in his film work. What's more striking, though, is that Lester's work makes something of a breakthrough in communicating the spirit of popular music in film. *It's Trad, Dad!* (1961) may seem an inauspicious debut for this approach, but the band performances within the film certainly show the music in its best light, and the excitement of a music craze comes across well.

This technique is developed further in *A Hard Day's Night* and *Help!* (1965), most notably with the musical sequences for 'Can't Buy Me Love' in the former film and 'Ticket to Ride' in the latter. This approach to pop music in cinema was a world away from earlier attempts. The music, here, dictates the image completely; it is not in the background, nor is it an aimless interlude with the performers spotlighted. Lester fits whichever image most suits the songs, thereby giving visual expression to the spirit of the songs.

Lester's later 1960s work intentionally breaks away from the musical associations he had formed. *The Knack* (1965), *Petulia* (1961), *How I Won The War* (1967) and *The Bed-Sitting Room* (1969) draw on elements buried within his earlier films: George Harrison's scene from *A Hard Day's Night* satirising fashion magazines, and the embittered scientists shorn of a grant from *Help!*, lead to these later, feature-length satires. Lester's television roots were surrealist comedy, and such instincts are given only limited rein in the Beatles' films, but become full-blown in *How I Won The War* and *The Bed-Sitting Room*.

Lester's career stalled in the early 1970s, before the successful release of *The Three Musketeers* (1973). Hereafter Lester's particular brand of comic-book mayhem comes to fruition. Lester's grounding in both comedy and advertising gives him a sure and novel grasp of fast editing, lending a frantic air of momentum to proceedings. Certainly this is seen in *A Hard Day's Night*: the Beatles are constantly in motion – even verbally – and the effect is breathlessly comic, to the point of becoming surreal. *Help!* takes the idea further, shot as it is in full colour. There is no pretence of documentary realism here, and the colourful locations and bizarre plot twists have the air of a three-colour comic book. Lester's subsequent 1960s work uses the inspired, fast editing and italicised style for darker, more satirical effect. *The Three Musketeers* (1973) and its two sequels, also use Lester's manic, comic energy to create pure adventure, again in a vaguely surreal, comic-book manner.

director as auteur

Lester's style is ideally suited to such fare, breathing life into the lives of colourful modern legends such as *Robin and Marian* (1976) and *Butch and Sundance: The Early Years* (1979). In turn this led to Lester working with a pop culture folk hero with *Superman II* (1980) and *Superman III* (1983). These sequels are the most successful of Lester's career, and clearly the comic-book character is a perfect vehicle for Lester's fascination with fast editing, colourful images and almost surreal humour.

Strikingly, Lester all but abandoned his vastly influential style of portraying pop music in cinema, despite being proclaimed as 'the father of MTV' (see Style: Soundtrack).

narrative & form

The narrative system employed within *A Hard Day's Night* is a common one: a day in the life. (In point of fact the film covers more than one day – actually around thirty-six hours.) From the opening shot when we see the Beatles escaping their fans and boarding a train, the narrative moves at a breakneck pace. Within this tightly conceived structure the narrative develops around the claustrophobic lifestyle of the Fab Four who have become prisoners of their own success.

As the narrative unfolds, we witness the Beatles employing a number of strategies to avoid their celebrity, and their screaming fans. At the level of story, however, apart from the fact that the four spend most of their time trying to avoid their fans, little else occurs. The writer, Alun Owen, wanted the film quite simply to be about the Beatles and their lifestyle. He was keen to represent their reality as faithfully as he could – to have it 'established right at the start with dozens, scores, hundreds of fans chasing the boys' (Walker, 1974, p. 237).

The narrative in *A Hard Day's Night* is tightly structured around the movement of the Beatles. At all times, the Fab Four are on the move. Whether it is escaping the hordes of fans, boarding the train, getting into a taxi, getting out of a taxi, going to the casino, arriving at the studio; they are always on the move. Always being on the move, without opportunity to escape the fans, reinforces the feeling of claustrophobia which is ever present within the film (see Themes). At the moment when the boys manage to escape the clutches of the fans, they literally break free from the studio, through a fire escape and out on to a field: at which point Ringo tellingly shouts 'We're out'. The scene is central to the film's dynamic, providing a respite for the Beatles as well as the audience. It provides an opportunity to sit back and relish the joyfulness and the sense of being carefree which follows as the Beatles cavort around a field as 'Can't Buy Me Love' plays non-diegetically on the soundtrack (see Style: Soundtrack).

This is also important stylistically, due to its innovative use of music and visuals (see Style).

As with any narrative, *A Hard Day's Night* operates around a system of cause and effect: that is, something happens which causes something else to happen. Additionally, a narrative is placed within time and space: something happens at a certain moment at a specific time within a particular location or setting. Specifically, the time and space of *A Hard Day's Night* is a television studio in contemporary London for a period of thirty-six hours.

The characters within a narrative most often cause its developments and problems. Within *A Hard Day's Night* it is Paul's Grandfather who is the foremost agent of cause and effect. Initially he comes along with the boys because he has a broken heart and Paul's mother thinks the trip will do him good. His unpleasantness towards Ringo results in the drummer disappearing just before the boys are due to perform. Similarly when they arrive at their hotel room he creates anxiety by going off to a casino and running up a large bill.

Paul's Grandfather isn't the only character in *A Hard Day's Night* to create obstructions within the narrative. Ringo's solitary walk through early morning London also creates problems: his disappearance sends the studio manager into a panic that he isn't going to have all four Beatles together for the performance.

Equally, however, things can occur within a film which neither impact on the narrative nor move it on. Instead they have some other function, for instance to give the audience further insight into a character, or to explore a particular theme in the film. When George goes into the advertising agency his actions don't advance the narrative. They do, however, make a number of interesting and insightful comments about the superficial nature of the fashion and advertising industries: witness the desperate desire by the advertising executive to have his finger on the pulse. This has further relevance: it also enhances George's character, revealing what a dry and witty young man he is, as well as situating the film in time and space via the would-be young and fashionable slang used by the desperate ad man.

Time is also crucial within *A Hard Day's Night*'s narrative. A film's time frame, whether it is the year in which the film is set, or the passing of a day, a month or a year, can be signalled in a number of ways. Inter-titles at the bottom of the screen may reveal that it is one year later, or a clock on the wall can signify that five minutes has passed. In the case of *A Hard Day's Night*, the fact that the film is tightly structured, with all the action taking place over thirty-six hours, means that time is vital and therefore referred to often. The audience needs this information to engage with the narrative. This particularly comes to the fore as the clock ticks away the anxious moments before the hour of the Beatles' performance. Ringo is still nowhere to be found, and the studio manager is losing patience.

A Hard Day's Night is a contemporary film, and the various spaces in which the film takes place are clearly recognisable as early 1960s Britain. There are various signifiers: witness the characters' clothes, their hairstyles and the language they use.

The look of the buildings and the general iconography all indicate to the audience that this is a film set during the same period in which it was made. Although it might seem dated to today's audiences, at the time it would have looked very modern indeed (see Costume).

There are a couple of brief moments when the film takes a non-conformist attitude to both time and space. When the Beatles are on the train, we see them one minute inside the carriage and the next outside banging on the window. This slightly surreal interlude prepares the audience for the next scene when the Beatles are playing cards in the luggage compartment one moment and the next instruments have appeared and they are singing 'I Should Have Known Better'. This playing with time and space also serves to remind us that we are not watching a documentary film about the Beatles (see Style).

characters

A Hard Day's Night has an advantage over many films: the four main characters – the Beatles – are already very well known. It is not so important to spend time setting up their characters, or developing their fictional personalities. Most of the audience will be familiar with them already. Of course, this could have worked to the film's disadvantage, if the writer and director had chosen to make a film in which the four played against type. Interestingly, despite the audience's prior familiarity with the Beatles, the film goes on to develop their personalities further. *A Hard Day's Night* goes to some lengths to establish them as individuals, rather than one four-headed group entity. Each Beatle is given his own starring scene. By highlighting each Beatle's individuality, the film offers its audience a range of personalities with which to empathise.

A film character can be active or passive, major or minor within the story. It is characters and their desires which generate cause and effect within a film: 'narrative invariably centres on personal psychological causes: decisions, choices and traits of characters' (Bordwell and Thompson, 1993, p. 68). *A Hard Day's Night*'s main characters are obviously John, Paul, George and Ringo. Supporting them are Paul's Grandfather, their road manager, Norm, and his assistant Shake.

As already noted, the film deliberately sets out to present the Beatles as individuals with recognisable personalities and character traits, and to this end, each of the Beatles has his own 'starring' scene. The film played on the idea that each member of the group would appeal to different members of the public. For instance, John Lennon's sarcasm was more appealing to the older fans; Paul McCartney was popular with the girls, whilst Ringo's humour had broader appeal. It was decided early on that there should be no love interest for any of the Beatles within the film. It was important for their image that they were seen as eligible bachelors. This again differs from Elvis Presley or Cliff Richard's pop films, where it was crucial for the heart-throbs to be romantically linked within the film, asserting their heterosexuality. (Ironically, George Harrison nevertheless met his future wife on the film – Patti Boyd, who plays one of the school girls on the train.)

Despite the fact that the film purports to show the 'real' Beatles, the film was tightly scripted and only slightly ad-libbed. Writer Owen's close-hand experience of the Beatles resulted in characterisations based on careful observation.

restless young men

Despite identifying the Beatles as individuals, there are some characteristics which are common to all four. They are restless young men, always on the move, and difficult to keep in one place for very long. As a group there has to be some sense of a shared identity which makes them recognisable as belonging to one another. The clothes they wear, their haircuts and their speech are all signifiers of this unity.

From the perspective of the Beatles' management and the film's financial backers, the film was important in crystallising the Beatles' characters for the public. It was the public's first real exposure to the four as individuals. Their record company thought that they would be a short-lived phenomenon, and saw *A Hard Day's Night* as a means of cashing-in on their success, and potentially elongating their popularity. The film's 'spotlighting' of the four Beatles in turn managed to deepen the public's fascination with the band. Aside from cashing-in on Beatlemania, *A Hard Day's Night* actually added depth to the band's image and helped secure their future longevity.

The Beatles had a real life outside of the world of the film, and it is therefore crucial that *A Hard Day's Night* is fiction (albeit based in fact), and not a documentary. Here, John, Paul, George and Ringo become characters in a film.

JOHN

John is the leader of the group – although his leadership manifests itself in subtle ways. He'd rather be cracking dirty jokes or chatting up school girls than discussing anything serious with the management. He is usually seen to be engaging in tomfoolery. His comic antics and surreal behaviour usually have an undermining effect on the older characters and authority figures in the film. The gentleman on the train and the television director both find themselves on the receiving end of John's withering sense of humour.

John has the least to do in the film, and he seems a little anonymous. Very little is revealed about him. His 'starring' scene is short, revolving around an actress who isn't sure whether he is who she thinks he is. His comic antics mask his real character, and as such John remains an enigmatic and intriguing figure.

PAUL

Paul is very much the clean-cut Beatle and the family man. He doesn't mind that his grandfather is accompanying him to London and he takes his responsibilities as a grandson seriously – although there is a clear inversion of roles, as Paul takes on the role of guardian. Paul isn't unduly concerned that he must keep his Grandfather away from mischief. A further reference to Paul's tight-knit family comes when George refers to Paul's other grandfather living at the family home.

Although Paul McCartney was occasionally dubbed the 'star' of the Beatles, the fictional Paul is the least well defined of the four within the film. Unfortunately for Paul's fans, his 'starring' sequence was cut from the finished film. The screenplay reveals that Paul wanders into a rehearsal room where a young actress is practising her lines. In the scene, Paul's urbane quality and sophistication show through, as he not only recognises the play, but also makes suggestions to the girl of how she might act out a particular scene. It is rumoured that the scene was cut, not, as the filmmakers have asserted, because it didn't fit within the film, but because Paul McCartney's acting in the scene was substandard.

It is within the music sequences that Paul displays the most confidence. As the band's lead vocalist he is usually centre stage and this particular role he carries well.

RINGO

Ringo is the most well-developed character within the film. This is largely due to his being the largest 'starring' scene of the four – and it also has real plot significance. The film's denouement hinges on Ringo. The scene also reveals subtle depths to Ringo's character, presenting him as multilayered: charming and vulnerable. He isn't just an ebullient pop star, and he isn't afraid to display his melancholy as he walks wistfully along the river bank. He is also childlike, both in his sense of humour and in his ability to readily engage with the young lad he meets on his walk.

Ringo is picked on by the other Beatles. They make fun of his nose, describing it as a 'trombone hooter' and they send him up for not receiving any fan mail. Even when Shake arrives with a huge pile of post for him, John has a dig at him saying 'That must have cost you a fortune in stamps, Ring'.

Ringo takes all this ribbing with good humour. He is the least precious of the four and the one least affected by his star status. This is borne out by his being happy to don down-at-heel clothes and disappear for a while. Also, when an attractive woman on the train beckons him to join her, he comically looks behind himself as if to find who she's beckoning. (Starr the actor even momentarily comes out of character during the press conference.)

GEORGE

George comes across as the most innocent of the Beatles. During his scene at the advertising agency, his naiveté is clearly present in his earnest responses to the risible requests of the advertising executive. Although not one of the chief members of the band, meaning singer/songwriters Lennon and McCartney, George nevertheless takes a back seat with dignity. He is never prone to the sometimes disruptive behaviour that Ringo displays. George is reliable and steadfast. He never causes any problems or upsets any characters in *A Hard Day's Night*.

GRANDFATHER

The role of Paul's Grandfather is an unusual one, and he is very much the foremost character in the film after the Beatles themselves. In this respect, it could be argued that this makes his the most potent role of all, since the Beatles are non-actors playing themselves, with dialogue intentionally written so as not to demand much of them. Additionally, each Beatle has just one 'showcase' solo scene. It's very much to Wilfred Brambell's credit that such a crucial role as the Grandfather works well, and is indeed entertaining and memorable.

the Grandfather fulfils a dramatic need

In essence, the Grandfather exists as a plot device within *A Hard Day's Night*. In the film, the Beatles are a unit, occasionally acting to frustrate their manager Norm, but most often behaving as they ought to. The Grandfather, however, travels within the Beatles' entourage, directly related to Paul. (Oddly, Paul's relationship with him isn't explored further in the film.) True to his reputation as 'a king mixer', the Grandfather stirs up dissent and anxiety within the ranks of the band, and hence instigates the dramatic situations in the film. He absconds to the casino with Ringo's invitation, necessitating that the band come to drag him away; he creates a running feud between the TV director and the band with a few well-chosen slights; he even persuades Ringo to go AWOL, 'parading' on the streets of London rather than sitting tight in the TV studio. The climactic police chase is caused directly by the Grandfather running from the police station: the police have no desire to put him on a charge, and follow only to return his signed photographs.

As such the Grandfather fulfils a dramatic need within the film by creating difficulties for the band. He also presents an interesting viewpoint on the Beatles. At a time when the four young men are worshipped by young girls the world over, the only figure shown to have penetrated their inner sanctum is an old man, with no interest in the band or their music.

The fact that the Grandfather turns out to be an interfering troublemaker is a neat reversal of the usual generation gap argument. The baby boomer Beatles are decent and well meaning, but the representative of the older generation in their midst is far less law-abiding. Undoubtedly this approach would appeal to the Beatles' younger fans, but arguably it also shows older audiences that this new pop band are, in fact, funny and decent people. The net effect of *A Hard Day's Night* was to widen the Beatles' appeal, by reaching older audiences and garnering serious appreciation. At least in part, this is an effect of the light cast on the band members by the Grandfather's behaviour.

reversal of stereotype

NORM

Long-suffering Norm has a strong dramatic function in *A Hard Day's Night*. Not quite the film's antagonist, it is nevertheless Norm's purpose as the Beatles' manager to frustrate their profound longing for freedom, and instead to focus their energies on the demands on their career. Needless to say, this attitude is essentially in the best interests of the band themselves: they aren't enslaved. But for the purposes of the film, within which imprisonment is such a major theme (see Themes), it is necessary that Norm enforces discipline on the unruly band. Norm is therefore seen chiding the Beatles into chores such as answering fan mail and rehearsing for the television performance. When the band members go missing, Norm endeavours to find them.

In an interesting reversal of stereotype, though, Norm is far from a cliché wheeler-dealer pop manager. His attitude towards his charges, although restrictive, is basically benevolent. In fact, Norm is almost unbelievably reliable and honest, and acts as a friend to the Beatles. Overall, although Norm plays out his role within the film perfectly, and provides fine entertainment with his love-cum-hate of the band (particularly John), the character suffers precisely because none of the film's characters develop beyond neat sketches. Perhaps this could be seen as intentional; since the Beatles were non-actors with only basic personalities in the film, all the supporting characters must by necessity measure up as rather thin. (It's striking, though, that although the Beatles appear as themselves, their real-life manager, Brian Epstein is absent from *A Hard Day's Night*.) Strangely, the character Norm who plays the manager role in the film is played by Norman Rossington; this playing with names to blur the division of fiction and reality is typical of *A Hard Day's Night*.

SHAKE

Shake too has a precise purpose within *A Hard Day's Night*, slotting exactly into the infrastructure of supporting characters. Shake is manager Norm's assistant, but speaks with a Liverpool accent and less chiding authority than Norm. As such Shake is a go-between for Norm and the band. If anything, Shake displays more affinity with the band than their put-upon manager. (As writer Alun Owen observed the Beatles and their inner circle on tour as research for the film, Shake surely has his roots in real-life Beatles' friends-turned-tour assistants such as Mal Evans and Neil Aspinall. Indeed, the first draft of the screenplay sees Norm called Neil and Shake called Mal.)

Shake has little of import to do within the plot of *A Hard Day's Night* but he provides Norm with a side-kick and sparring partner (most obviously with the running joke between them about Shake's height). Quite obviously, the Beatles' real-life business life would have required the work of more than two men, but here Shake, alongside Norm, stands in for such numerous figures. Shake gets to bond with George as the latter teaches him how to shave (marking him out as being rather inexperienced), and clowns alongside the band, much to Norm's chagrin. Curiously, 'Shake' sounds like a nickname, but at no point is any explanation for this put forward.

TV DIRECTOR

Within the rather thin plot of *A Hard Day's Night*, the Director is the foremost antagonist to the lead characters – although strictly speaking the Beatles are more correctly the Director's antagonists, since they create obstacles to frustrate him in his goals, rather than vice versa. But the Director is certainly the bands' opposite number, representing all that they are not: he is tense, negative, older and closed-minded, with a strong sense of paranoia. (Oddly the Beatles themselves never suspect that anyone means them any actual harm, and in the whole film they are never put in any remotely threatening situations.)

As with Norm and Shake, the Director stands in for an entire industry: he provides mass consumption light entertainment, for a more old-fashioned generation than that which spawned the Beatles. As with Norm, the Director has a younger, less serious assistant within the TV studio; and the Director too must face the whims of the Beatles, the very force he is trying to harness and broadcast with a minimum of personal stress. The Director's highly strung, world-weary manner provides some fine comic moments within the film. In addition, it's notable that both Richard Lester and Alun Owen had worked extensively in popular television (far more so than in film) before making *A Hard Day's Night*. As such, the television director with shredded nerves is surely a figure both knew well – and in Lester's case, had perhaps actually been!

themes

Part of *A Hard Day's Night*'s enduring appeal is the fact that, whilst planned as an economic pop **exploitation** feature, the finished product actually contains strong and developed themes. The makers of the film not only capture the Beatlemania phenomenon on film, but also skilfully comment on it.

REALITY VERSUS IMAGE

The film was sold to the band's adoring fans as a window into the lives of their idols. But cinema, of course, cannot offer reality: only an impressionistic simulacrum of it. Richard Lester and Alun Owen are canny enough not only to recognise this, but also make full use of it. Throughout *A Hard Day's Night* we are reminded that this is in no way reality; the gulf between reality and a fabricated image is referred to subtly yet constantly.

Certainly Lester, a devotee of the French New Wave (see Style), was enamoured of *cinéma vérité* techniques such as hand-held cameras, and he was dedicated to capturing the raw flavour of the Beatles' odd existence. Recalling also that an early working title for the film was 'Beatlemania', the title sequence has a frantic documentary feel not unlike news footage of the day concerning the Beatles phenomenon.

Once on board the train to London, we see that the Beatles are playing themselves in the film, in situations that were common to them. But as they themselves remark, a stranger is in their midst; the fictional figure of Paul's Grandfather. Not only that, but Wilfred Brambell would be familiar to British audiences as a popular character actor (see Biographies). At this precise point, reality is left behind, both for the Beatles and the viewing audience. All have entered a cinematic world touched by fantasy and creative licence.

themes

Thirteen minutes into the film, the Beatles break into a performance of their song 'I Should Have Known Better'. In itself, this is far from average behaviour for real people. In this instance, though, director Lester dispenses with the traditional form of pop songs in cinema. Previous stars such as Elvis Presley and Cliff Richard would perform songs to a musical backing provided by musicians seen on screen, or else the songs would have some narrative purpose, thereby expressing some inner feelings of the performer (see Soundtrack). The presentation of songs in *A Hard Day's Night* is no more 'real' than any previous cinematic attempt, but at points it dispenses with any illusion of performance. During the 'Can't Buy Me Love' sequence, the Beatles' movements are actually exaggerated and speeded up. In just over half an hour, the film has moved from documentary realism to almost surreal expressionism.

Lester's intentions with such techniques may be to communicate the raw truth of the Beatles' experience in a manner more expressionist, more subliminal, than simple documentary. Surely, for instance, a life spent speeding from one hotel room to another would barely feel real at all. Accordingly, the brief sequence in the hotel bathroom features two surreal incidents: George teaches Shake to shave by spraying foam, not onto his face, but onto the reflection of his face in the mirror. An image of George stands in for the real thing; this device will recur later. Meanwhile, John disappears from the draining bath, defying the laws of science, leading Norm to believe he's met some bizarre fate. In the unnatural setting of a hotel bathroom, nature itself suspends its laws.

The film moves on to its setting of a television studio. This in itself is telling, for the studio is a symbol of the manufactured image, designed solely to create the illusory image. Repeatedly the Beatles are seen, not directly, but on studio monitor screens. The band enter onto the stage at one point to find an old-fashioned dance troupe performing to an easy-listening version of the band's song 'I'm Happy Just to Dance With You'. The band burst into a thrilling live version of the song, utterly at odds with the light entertainment version just witnessed. This live version is shown initially through the viewfinder of the studio camera – hence, an image of the band, rather than the band themselves. The Beatles are, clearly, not the old guard of song-and-dance variety performers; but for all their freshness, they are at the mercy of how the media presents them. Much as they try, their public image is a monster beyond their control. Indeed, during the course of *A Hard Day's Night* the Beatles' characters expend as much energy thwarting the effects of fame as they do fanning the flames of their career. (In a curious twist of fate, the real life Beatles came to detest the image even more, George Harrison in particular resenting being branded 'ex-Beatle' for the rest of his life.)

Each Beatle plays truant from the television rehearsals to have a solo adventure. John Lennon is seen being stopped by Millie, a woman who is convinced she knows his identity. 'You are, I know you are ...' she exclaims, only for John to deny it. Tellingly, performers in full costume rush about in the background as the scene plays. 'Well, you look like him ...' insists Millie. Games are being played with image and identity. The pair even examine John's reflection – that is, his image – in a mirror, echoing George's shaving scene in the hotel bathroom. But when Millie concurs 'You don't look like him at all', John seems most insulted. He may fear the curse of a celebrity identity, but he wouldn't like to entirely lose it.

Meanwhile, George strays into a fashion editor's office. Without a word, he is mistaken for 'a good type ... a real one' – that is, someone in the style of the Beatles. George is taken to be an approximation of his own image, rather than the genuine article. The scene is *A Hard Day's Night*'s most outright attempt at satire. In the flesh, the fashion professionals can't tell George from his image – or else, they aren't familiar enough with the real Beatles to identify one. Again, this compares directly to George 'shaving' his own reflection. To the characters in the film, the Beatles' fabricated images are more real than the actual Beatles.

In Ringo's jaunt outside, he is first pursued by screaming fans. He must mask his identity by swiftly changing into unfamiliar junk shop clothes. Once his image has been altered, he is free to walk untroubled. His only encounter, though, is with a little boy – hardly the core of the Beatles'

a piece of Beatles merchandising

audience – to whom Ringo is a stranger, and who is happiest talking about himself and his friends.

A Hard Day's Night wilfully toys with these notions of identity – in particular mistaken identity – and the manufactured image of the Beatles. By posing as a documentary, the film promises the truth about the band. It's no coincidence though that it features an exchange between Norm and John, where Norm threatens to tell the 'truth' about John.

Tellingly, this dialogue is between John Lennon (playing himself) and actor Norman Rossington (playing the role of the Beatles' road manager, although he didn't actually take that role in reality!). The truth, it tells us, is something we can't be told. The film subtly highlights the fact that the Beatles' public personae are a creation, quite detached from their actual personalities. The film, too, is at heart a piece of Beatles merchandising, rather than 'the truth'. Even Paul's own Grandfather, who shows no interest in the band members themselves, despite having full access to them, is not above hawking covertly signed photos of them to their fans. The film's final image is of the band ascending to the skies by helicopter, more like modern day gods than humble humans; and as they do so, they cast out Grandfather's signed photos to flutter down to the ground. The photographic images of the Beatles – smiling, perfectly groomed and wholly acceptable – are thrown away by the band themselves, symbolically discarding their public personae. Of course, that hasn't happened in the film itself: if anything, they've played basic caricatures of themselves as their public expects them to be. But throughout, games are played with the Beatles' image.

IMPRISONMENT

The Beatles weren't the first musicians to be idolised by their fans. Even classical composers were said to have caused the women in their audiences to scream uncontrollably. In recent times, swing singer Frank Sinatra afforded rapturous responses from hordes of adoring 'bobbysoxers' in the 1940s. Elvis Presley, one of rock 'n' roll's progenitors, was also idolised en masse by teenage girl fans. Despite these precedents,

the Beatlemania phenomenon was extraordinary

though, the Beatlemania phenomenon was simply extraordinary. Such was the intensity of their fans that it wasn't possible for the band to openly meet them and bask in the glory of adulation. In public, the band risked being mobbed, and were in actual physical danger. As we see from the opening shots of *A Hard Day's Night*, the only reasonable action the band could take was to flee from their fans as fast as possible. Certainly this is an odd reaction to the fruits of their success: but in fact the Beatles were trapped – often physically – by the result of their celebrity.

In the film, Paul's Grandfather is heard to complain 'I thought I was going to get a change of scenery and so far I've been in a train and a room and a car and a room and a room and a room'. Supposedly this line was overheard by scriptwriter Alun Owen during his period spent researching with the band themselves. In *A Hard Day's Night* Owen and director Lester turn this confinement to their advantage, and highlight the predicament that the Beatles' success has caused. (There is an obvious practical advantage in taking this approach, too, in terms of grounding the film in small, economic sets.) Once the band have boarded the train during the film's opening scenes, having escaped their fans at top speed, they resemble prisoners being 'transported' from cell to cell under the watch of Norm and Shake, effectively their jailers. This is highlighted when the Grandfather claims to two girls that they are indeed 'prisoners'. The band resent the implication, but later John play-acts the prisoner role to the girls, yelling 'I won't go back ... I bet you can guess what I was in for'.

The first song performed in the film, 'I Should Have Known Better', takes place in a guards van with the band encaged. In this 'imprisoned' environment, the band fall into performing. Throughout *A Hard Day's Night* the band have a curious relationship with their music. The vast success of their music has caused them to be hunted by fans, unable to walk freely outdoors; to be prisoners of their own success. Yet here they turn to music as a form of escapism, and freedom. Possibly this is meant as an expressionistic device, illustrating the freedom of spirit that can be caused by creative expression. Certainly, the Beatles' songs are used within the film to highlight moments in which their imprisonment is thrown into sharp relief. The band escape the watchful glare of Norm to go from the hotel to a nightclub. They dance, temporarily free, to the sound of their own songs – until jailer Norm comes to get them. (Later, when the band disappear again, a weary Norm says 'I've considered a ball and chain ...')

A pivotal scene here is the 'Can't Buy Me Love' sequence. Diving through a fire exit, the band run about madly in an empty field. It's a simple pleasure, but one that the band have become unused to. Free from marauding fans, strict road managers or demanding TV directors, the band are, for one moment, free to be together. In this respect it's plain that there is a direct connection between the Beatles' freedom and their music. The lyrics of 'Can't Buy Me Love' bear no relation to the scene, or anything within the film's plot. But symbolically, the band 'run free' and their music starts. As before, the magic of the Beatles' music is in the sound of the band 'running free' creatively. What they create when they're together sets them free. (Tellingly, the moments the band members have when they roam free from their constraints individually are far less magical. Each seems lost and lonely. The magic of the band, and their spiritual freedom, relies upon their unity as a group.)

The film continues to juxtapose scenes of virtual imprisonment with those of music-making freedom. Images recur of literal restraint: the errant Grandfather is handcuffed and taken to a police station. Trapped in the television studio, the band break into making music to relieve the boredom. A chase sequence occurs at the story's end when the police pursue the Grandfather and Ringo through the streets (echoing the chase at the film's opening when the band flee their fans). But the film's finale comes, as might be expected, with a long live performance by the Beatles (for the television show). This only becomes possible when Ringo returns to the fold. Ringo's individual journey towards the live performance is very illuminating. He is goaded into leaving the studio by the troublemaking Grandfather, with talk of 'parading'. In fact, Ringo goes out only to find himself recognised by adoring fans. He disguises himself, and becomes lonely. He encounters a young boy playing by the river. Like Ringo, the boy is playing truant. The boy doesn't recognise the pop star, seeming more interested in talking about himself and his friends. Ringo wistfully watches the boy return to his three male playmates.

Just as Ringo parallels the young boy, the boy and his friends represent the Beatles. Ringo isn't made free by 'parading' the streets. His freedom lies in his life as a Beatle, 'playing' with his friends. Shortly, Ringo is arrested for his behaviour in the bar, before becoming reunited with his fellow Beatles. In the finale, the band are at last free to play their music at length, delighting their screaming fans, and making themselves smile in the process. The final image is of a helicopter carrying the band into the sky: an image evocative of freedom, and paralleling the euphoric high (of the non-chemical variety!) that the band would experience after a performance. The symbolic imprisonment the band have suffered throughout *A Hard Day's Night* is temporarily relieved by their music-making throughout, and their eventual 'escape' is itself caused by their creativity.

THE GENERATION GAP

The post-Second World War baby boom resulted in a huge youth population in Britain, all approaching adulthood in the early 1960s. This created a good deal of conflict between the older generation (who had lived through a war and its attendant hardships) and the younger generation (who loathed postwar austerity, craved change and had newly found strength in numbers). The generational conflict was therefore key to the pop music film, but attempts to depict it prior to *A Hard Day's Night* had been lacklustre. A typical example would be the Cliff Richard vehicle *The Young Ones* (1961). This features teen pop idol Richard as Nicky, a talented youngster who anonymously records a song to raise funds for his local youth club, which faces redevelopment by an unscrupulous property tycoon. However, Nicky keeps a secret from his young friends: the tycoon is his own father. Hence the older generation is set up as amoral and greedy, giving reign to selfish, destructive urges, even though they conflict directly with the harmless, creative instincts of the younger generation.

In *A Hard Day's Night* the portrayal of the generation gap is far less hysterical and cartoonish. The first contact the Beatles have with the older generation comes soon after the titles, in a railway carriage. The bowler-hatted commuter they encounter is among the few characters in the film not to recognise the band on sight. Their treatment of the older man is, whilst playful, unstintingly polite. His behaviour towards them, however, is dismissive and domineering: he insists that they turn off their radio and close the carriage window (even though, as John points out, 'There's more of us than there is of you'). The band remain reasonable throughout, with the gent growing increasingly territorial. He quickly resorts to such clichés as 'I fought a war for the likes of you!', causing the band to desert the carriage with John saying dryly, 'It's your carriage, isn't it, Mister?'. This scene is the closest *A Hard Day's Night* comes to the traditional conflicts of the likes of *The Young Ones*. But whereas the earlier film seems tailor-made for young audiences, depicting the older generation as mean and negative, *A Hard Day's Night* shows the younger generation themselves in a particularly decent and favourable light. As a result, it became something of a turning point in the band's career, whereafter more mature audiences began to appreciate the band and their music. This is a subtle inversion of the generational issues from *The Young Ones*. In the Cliff Richard movie, the youthful leads come to conquer their oppressive elders. In this scene from *A Hard Day's Night*, the Beatles simply walk away and leave the stuffy gent to it. This outright rejection of the older generation's values is a small premonition of the independent youth movements such as the 'flower people' of the later 1960s.

The film's most prominent representative of the mature generation is of course Paul's Grandfather. But far from being a beacon of senior wisdom, the Grandfather is an outright troublemaker who needs the band to chaperone him. In fact the Grandfather – insulting, problematic, moody and difficult to control – is far more of a child than the band members. Although Norm has to extricate the Beatles from situations during the film, the larger problems are caused by the Grandfather and the band are left to sort them out. Apart from the humour inherent in this inversion of the norm, there's undoubted intent in the Beatles being leading the country to ruin

portrayed as the responsible party and the Grandfather being the troublesome fly in the ointment. The younger generation, we are told, aren't necessarily difficult and ill-meaning as the older generation may think. They are in fact capable of being decent and helpful, and their elders are just as capable of mischief. In one telling moment, John dons a false beard and proclaims that the older generation are leading the country to ruin. By taking on the appearance of an older man, John inverts accepted wisdom about the generational conflict, and turns a cliché on its head. At another point, John is also heard to grab a guitar in the studio, and ironically suggest that they do the show right there – a stock phrase from those aforementioned previous youth pictures with less sophisticated approaches to the generation.

Another elder-but-not-better of the Beatles is the neurotic TV director. Charged with marshalling the band into their television appearance, he can barely function for anxiety, self-loathing and paranoia (see Narrative and Form: Characters). He is sure that the whole interlude is a plot and complains about the pressure of his job. In practice, he isn't at all efficient. The show goes ahead by the skin of his teeth, and when the Grandfather pops from under the stage during rehearsals of an opera piece, the Director's reaction is vague: he isn't quite sure whether it is wrong or not. He is an ineffectual bag of neuroses. The Beatles are, by comparison, extremely together personalities, and for all their wayward urges, they are consummate professionals, fully in control of their own creative powers. Again, they as young men show up their elders as being far from their betters.

The Beatles' one unshackled moment is the 'Can't Buy Me Love' sequence, in which they run freely in the outdoors. But the sequence is brought to a close when they are discovered by the owner of the field, who shouts 'I suppose you know this is private property?'. Their fun curtailed, the Beatles slope off, and George dryly replies 'Sorry if we hurt your field, Mister'. This echoes the railway carriage encounter with the businessman. Again the older generation mean-spiritedly foils the young Beatles' fun, and the band's parting shot is to dryly point up the possessiveness of the gesture. The effect can be comic, but it's also pointed. *A Hard Day's Night*

effect on both the music scene and the world's media

enters the arena of the generation-gap pop movie, but with a level of sophistication and sly, knowing wit that previous versions of the formula couldn't muster. (This too reflects the general effect that the Beatles had on both the music scene and the world's media. Their barbed humour made an impact in many spheres.) The Beatles aren't portrayed as simple-minded do-gooder victims as youths had been before. They are more complex, capable of both exasperating mischief and surprising kindness. By leading the genre out of its one-dimensional rut, *A Hard Day's Night* emerges as a subtle commentary on the generationally divided society in which it was made, using an unusual array of older and younger people to make points about the issue.

parallelism

Whilst watching a film we may notice images or situations which we have already seen in the film, or comparison may be drawn between two or more elements. This process is called parallelism. There are numerous examples in *A Hard Day's Night*, with many of them referring to real events in the Beatles' lives. The press conference for example parallels the Beatles own surreal responses to inane questions at press conferences.

Additionally, Paul's Grandfather is constantly referred to as being very clean – a reference to actor Wilfred Brambell's 'dirty old man' character in the TV series *Steptoe and Son* (see Background: Biographies). A filmic example comes when Ringo plays 'truant' from the band, only to meet up with some children also playing truant (from school).

Parallelism can also function stylistically. By highlighting the similar, the film invites the viewer to compare distinct elements, and in doing so helps with our understanding of the film:

> we must be able to recall and identify characters and settings each time they reappear. More subtly, throughout any film we can observe repetitions of everything from lines of dialogue and bits of music to camera positions, characters' behaviour and story action.
>
> *Bordwell and Thompson, 1993, p. 57*

not all plot lines will be developed

opening/closing

By comparing the beginning and the ending of a film, we often find that the film's journey has come full circle. Characters' desires have been met, plot lines have been explored, some have been dropped along the way, and any questions which the film started out with have been answered. The opening of a film is particularly important in that it paves the way for what is to come. It sets up the action, where we are and when. In other words, it situates us within time and space: it brings us into the narrative: 'the opening raises our expectations by setting up a specific range of possible causes for and effects of what we see' (Bordwell and Thompson, 1993, p. 73). Plot lines established at the beginning of a film set the audience's expectations about what the film is going to be about. However, not all plot lines will be developed and as the plot develops: 'the causes and effects will define narrower patterns of development' (Bordwell and Thompson, 1993, p. 73).

In comparing the beginning and end of *A Hard Day's Night*, we can see that the Beatles begin the film running away from their fans, and the final shot is of them fleeing yet again, this time by helicopter. The band have overcome all emergent obstacles to make their television appearance. They wander free of Norm, but are found. The Grandfather's troublemaking has been curbed, and the Fab Four are again on their way to another engagement at top speed.

style

There are three main influences on the cinematic style of *A Hard Day's Night*: kitchen sink films, the French New Wave and the documentary. Richard Lester wanted *A Hard Day's Night* to have a naturalistic look. Although realism was the dominant mode of the so-called kitchen sink films, it was new territory for the pop film. The elements which help create this style are the mise-en-scène and the cinematography – shots, editing and so on. The camera work and the editing also encompass elements of another realist style of film making – the French New Wave. Characteristics typical of the French New Wave films are the use of natural light and hand-held cameras and location, rather than studio, filming.

French New Wave is a term applied to a number of films made in France in the late 1950s and early 1960s. The most famous exponents of the movement are François Truffaut and Jean-Luc Godard. The French New Wave style is also known as *cinéma vérité* because of its attempts to capture real life on camera. Many *cinéma vérité* effects can be seen in documentary making, particularly the use of black and white film stock, hand-held cameras and naturalistic lighting. Gilbert Taylor, the cinematographer on *A Hard Day's Night* was a devotee of the *cinéma vérité* style and he used it to great effect in the film. Richard Lester and Gilbert Taylor felt that directors like Godard in France and John Cassavetes in America were breaking new ground using light, 16mm hand-held cameras. These cameras brought a new, improvised quality reminiscent of documentary to the feature film. To shoot the film in black and white, one of the characteristics of both Nouvelle Vague and documentary making, was purely an artistic decision. The effect of shooting in black and white reinforces the feeling of actuality and lends the finished product a timelessness.

no narrative purpose

The film's narrative style is also influenced by the French New Wave - meandering and elusive. Like the French New Wave films, *A Hard Day's Night* contains narrative strands which do little to move the plot on, and the characters are not goal orientated. The majority of the Beatles' actions in the film serve no narrative purpose whatsoever.

The film's realism is strongly counteracted by several surreal moments in the film. From the outset the clues are there that this is not just a kitchen sink style film: 'the viewer's ability to perceive the action through a singularly realist aesthetic is constantly destabilised by the invasion of humorous surreal sequences and "moments" which constantly, yet unexpectedly, hijack the illusion of actuality and "surprise" the audience' (Neaverson, 1997, p. 184). The scene which epitomises the film's anti-realism most clearly is the celebrated 'Can't Buy Me Love' scene: 'Lester's film freed the representation of the musical number from its traditional generic slavery' (Neaverson, 1997, p. 19) (see Soundtrack).

mise-en-scène

Confusion often abounds over the term mise-en-scène. It was originally a theatrical direction which referred to everything which is put into a scene – props, set, actors etc. When the term is transferred to film analysis it implies everything within the frame – the lighting, the sets, props, actors, costumes: 'By extension from theatre to cinema, the term has come to mean the director's control over what appears in the frame, the way the director stages the event for the camera' (Cook, 1994, p. 191). Photographic qualities, such as the shot, camera position and editing are not part of the mise-en-scène.

Mise-en-scène analysis is useful in so far as it provides a practical way of reading a film. It is often linked with auteur theory in that auteurists argue that the sign of a true auteur is a director who is fully in control of the composition of their films as well as themes and values contained within them. An example of this type of director would be Alfred Hitchcock who had everything worked out on storyboards before shooting began.

mise-en-scène in a hard day's night

LOCATION

In general, British films at the time of *A Hard Day's Night* would be studio based. Outside location filming tended to be minimal and most often took place in London (close to the studio). Interestingly, however, with the rise of the so-called kitchen sink films (or the British New Wave as it is also known), location shooting did move north, as this is where most of these films were set. The British New Wave films set in the north of England include *A Taste of Honey*, *Saturday Night and Sunday Morning* (set in the Midlands) and *A Kind of Loving*. The majority of them were made between 1959 and 1963. It's interesting then, that *A Hard Day's Night*, which was made in 1964, begins with the four main characters leaving the north and heading south for a television appearance. Symbolically moving away from the grim and grimy north, familiar to cinema goers at the time, to London, 'swinging London' as it was becoming. The focus of the burgeoning youth culture scene of which the Beatles were a defining part.

A Hard Day's Night was made both on location and within a studio setting. Once again, due to budget constraints, the production schedule was tight. Filming took place in and around London for exteriors, and Twickenham studios for interior shots. It was an eight week shoot. Shooting outside at real locations was essential for the look of the film, but difficult logistically. The train route somehow got leaked resulting in fans bombarding the train, as associate producer Denis O'Dell remembers, 'kids would be jumping in front of the bloody train, so every day we would change the route because we couldn't get the Beatles on the train, never mind get to shoot' (Neaverson, 1997, p. 15).

The film has moments of authenticity provided by the street scenes as well as the controlled environment of the studio. The film begins with some location shooting as the Beatles are filmed running frantically down the street towards the train station and away from their screaming hordes of fans. This initial location shooting was shot using a hand-held camera which gives the scene a spontaneous, fast feel. There is a strong sense of the now – the film captured Beatlemania as it was happening.

Other outside location scenes include Ringo's walkabout, his interlude by the canal, scenes shot outside the television studio and most significantly, the scene when they literally break out of the studio, onto a field where they sing 'Can't Buy Me Love'. This scene is central to the film's dynamic. Up until this point, every scene in the film has been shot at close proximity. The Beatles' sense of confinement and claustrophobia is reinforced by the medium shots and close-ups used. In this sense the style reinforces the film's themes.

LIGHTING

Lighting in a film is very important and the whole impact that an image has very often comes from the way it is lit: 'lighting is more than just illumination that permits us to see the action' (Bordwell and Thompson, 1993, p. 152).

The lighting style within *A Hard Day's Night* is generally naturalistic – although on occasion there is a more experimental approach which is again at odds with the film's realist aesthetic and more in keeping with Lester's desire to be innovative. The natural light of the street scenes contrasts with the artificial studio lighting in which the light is seen to be going right through Paul as he performs on stage. This conflict between the naturalistic aspirations and the expressionist quality again reminds us that we are not watching a documentary but a feature film.

Lighting can be used in a variety of ways to achieve a variety of effects. Film lighting is an important aspect of the mise-en-scène and it can be used symbolically or to create atmosphere. *A Hard Day's Night* has a striking visual style which the lighting is instrumental in creating.

COSTUMES AND FASHION

The clothes worn in the film are contemporary. They represent early 1960s fashions for young people. The outfits worn by the Beatles in the film became synonymous with their 'look' – drain pipe trousers, turtle neck sweaters, mod-style jackets with thin lapels. It was a look which they themselves had made popular. It was a uniform for youth culture. It's also remarkable just how much the Beatles are identified by their look. When Ringo goes walkabout, he disguises himself in an old overcoat and cap which he picks up at a second hand clothes shop. He tests out his new anonymity on a passing female, who cries, 'Get out of it, short house!'

Female fashion of the time is also represented in *A Hard Day's Night*. In the nightclub scene early on in the film, young women are seen sporting winklepickers and beehive hairdos. Fashionable clothes and haircuts are the order of the day. Such contemporary fashions add to the documentary effect of the film. Once again, youth culture is contrasted with the conventional standards of the older people in the film. The man in the railway carriage carries a bowler hat with a three piece suit, the typical uniform of the white-collar worker. References to the Beatles' fashionable quality permeates the film. They are positioned as trendsetters and everyone takes their dress sense and sense of style very seriously. At the press conference there is considerable interest in the Beatles' hairstyles, and Ringo is even asked what he likes his girlfriends to wear. When George finds himself at the advertising agency, the manager is desperate for his opinion on some shirts. *A Hard Day's Night* captures the importance of fashion to young people in early 1960s British culture.

dialogue and performance

Alan Owen's script is one of the main agents of the film's naturalistic effect. However, although the film has an improvised quality, there are actually only a couple of lines which are ad-libbed. Having lived in Liverpool himself, Owen was able to accurately capture the Beatles' speech patterns. After spending a couple of days on tour with the Beatles he had their witty repartee down to a fine art: 'Owen's script, based on direct observation and populated by Spoonerisms, colloquialisms and

dialogue and performance style

Liverpool slang, lends the action such a unique sense of naturalism that it also creates a convincing illusion of reality' (Neaverson, 1997, p. 16).

Although the Beatles were undoubtedly acting in the film, they are to a large extent playing themselves. Unlike in an Elvis film where Elvis would take on the character of a racing car driver or a tour guide, the Beatles appear in *A Hard Day's Night* as embodiments of their public personae. The casting of Wilfred Brambell as Paul's Grandfather meant that there was a mainstay of English theatre, film and television in the cast. Such a household name provides an extra element to the film: in particular, older audiences would appreciate his presence. His reputation lends the film credibility. The Beatles themselves had never acted before, once again reinforcing the *cinéma vérité* style, as non-professional actors who help the film seem 'real'.

cinematography

A Hard Day's Night was made extremely quickly – partly because of budget restrictions and partly because nobody knew how long the Beatles phenomenon would last. This sense of urgency informs the film's documentary effect. Richard Lester worked with cinematographer Gilbert Taylor, as he had done on his earlier film *It's Trad Dad* (1961). Taylor was aware just how inventive black and white photography could be. He shared Lester's interest in the *cinéma vérité* style. They were inspired by French New Wave directors such as Jean-Luc Godard and American film maker John Cassavetes, both of whom were breaking new ground using light cameras to create an improvised style. Taylor was given quite a free reign by Lester, and in scenes like the 'Can't Buy Me Love' sequence reveals how a combination of spontaneity and inventiveness helped to create the look of the film, he says: 'when we came to do a shot from the helicopter, the battery I was handed for the hand-held camera wasn't fully charged – we started to shoot and the speed went down' (Walker, 1974, p. 240).

Other aspects to consider when discussing cinematography include: depth of field, framing, shot duration, camera angles. The film's musical sequences in particular show off the range of camera angles chosen to

sound and soundtrack

film the Beatles. They are shot from all sides: from above, below and sideways. The experimental approach to lighting complemented the camera work and the two together are key aspects of the film's style.

sound and soundtrack

The soundtrack to *A Hard Day's Night* is of course written and performed by the Beatles. Songs, most of which written specifically for the film, play diegetically and non-diegetically throughout the film. None of the songs in the film have any narrative purpose. They were not custom-written to fit certain slots, and the scriptwriter Alun Owen played no part in the songwriting. Instead the Beatles simply wrote a selection of new songs absolutely in their own style. The one exception is the title song, written in one night after Ringo Starr uttered the magical phrase and the film project was hastily re-christened (see Backgrounds: Making *A Hard Day's Night*). But although the film's title expresses the manic pace of the band's lifestyle, the song itself is a robust love song – as, in fact, are all seven of the film's songs. Such was the Beatles' style at the time; but there is no love interest in the film at all, and so the songs could not possibly play any narrative role.

Richard Lester uses the seven songs very differently. 'I Should Have Known Better' simply starts as the band play cards. Soon they are seen to mime along to the lyric, before switching to play their instruments too. It's perhaps the least successful of the songs in the film, with the change to 'performing' seeming clumsy. Perhaps, though, Lester is intentionally easing us into the full-blown stylistic leap he is about to take. The second song, 'If I Fell', is performed in the deserted television studio effectively 'to' a sulking Ringo 'by' John (who introduces the song with a gleeful cry of 'I'll show him!') although the song is clearly about a possible love affair.

There are however a couple of older Beatles songs (such as 'She Loves You', the Beatles biggest hit to date), included to engage existing fans who might not be happy hearing unfamiliar songs. The Beatles' music is used in the film in a manner which hadn't been seen in the pop film up to this point. In Cliff Richard films, or Elvis films, musical sequences strived to appear like genuine performances. Cliff or Elvis would be seen lip synching to their songs. In *A Hard Day's Night* there is no attempt to represent the musical sequences as real performances. Instead the songs aren't always tied to performance, most notably in the park sequence where: 'the group's antics are framed from self-consciously unconventional angles and at exaggeratedly artificial speeds' (Neaverson, 1997, p. 18). This pivotal third song 'Can't Buy Me Love' starts on the soundtrack at the very moment the Beatles escape into the outdoors. They proceed to gambol and play in the field, unattended, as the song plays. But at no point do they seem to sing or perform it – even though, amazingly, it is they that perform it as it plays. Equally, the subject of the song has nothing to do with the actions of the Beatles as it continues. Lester is communicating the energy and passion of the song in the attendant visuals, whilst dispensing with any pretence of on-screen performance. By allowing the Beatles to cavort freely whilst their song, 'Can't Buy Me Love', plays non-diegetically, Lester liberated the song from the conventional representation in pop films up to this point. Lester 'allowed the pop song the opportunity to work in a similar manner to conventional incidental music, as an abstract entity capable of punctuating action which is not performance orientated' (Neaverson, 1997, p. 19). Because of his radical new approach to presenting the pop song on film, Lester has subsequently been credited with inventing the pop video.

The film's later songs are presented in slightly less extraordinary a fashion, and there are times when songs are more traditionally represented in terms of performance. For instance, they play a number of songs in the television studio at the end of the film. Although Lester is quick to point out that the performance is still filmed much more unconventionally than would have been the norm, the cinematographer ensuring that a variety of techniques and unconventional camera angles were used to film the Beatles' performance of the musical numbers in the film.

The songs in the film run the whole gamut of the Beatles' repertoire. Ballads, love songs and rock 'n' roll numbers are all represented within the film. John, Paul and George all have a go at performing lead vocals in the film, whilst Ringo's vocal ability is heard on 'I Wanna Be Your Man' in the disco scene early on in the film. This ties in with the film's efforts to present the Beatles individually, exposing their unique talents and vocal ability. There were advanced sales of over two million copies, making it the biggest selling album ever. The film won an Academy Award nomination for Best Soundtrack.

BLACK AND WHITE

The fact that *A Hard Day's Night* is made in black and white is significant. It was certainly significant in 1963 when the film was made, since at this time more and more films were being made in colour. Thus it was a stylistic choice (although budget had some impact on the decision, too). Once again, Lester's admiration for the French New Wave was an influencing factor. Since then, the issue of black and white has come under a lot of discussion, and the general feeling is that if the film had of been made in colour it wouldn't have anything like the iconic status it enjoys today.

Several of Richard Lester's other films were shot in black and white, including *The Running, Jumping, Standing Still Film* – which had influenced the Beatles in their choice of Lester as director of their debut – as well as *It's Trad Dad*. Gilbert Taylor, Lester's cinematographer on the latter returned on *A Hard Day's Night* to innovate afresh with black and white photography.

The choice of black and white film added to the film's sense of realism, reminiscent of the British and French New Wave, although it was a realism which was broken up with moments of surrealism. The use of black and white brought audiences back down to earth, reminding them of gritty, realist dramas. For Lester, however, it was more of a stylistic statement than an attempt to make something gritty.

EDITING

Editing is essential to a film's logic. The way shots are ordered makes a film readable: 'editing functions both to move the story along and also, through the precise juxtaposition of shots, to constitute the causal logic

sound and soundtrack

ellipses of time are common in art cinema

of narrative events' (Cook, 1994, p. 213). When the editing doesn't follow this convention and instead juxtaposes two unrelated shots, events take on a more surreal logic. In classical narrative cinema, it is essential that the editing appears seamless: this is known as continuity editing. Different shot types are edited so as to direct the viewer into the story. Typically there will be an establishing shot, followed by a close-up, followed by a longer shot to re-establish where the action is taking place. *A Hard Day's Night* has some features of classical Hollywood narrative combined with more of an art cinema aesthetic (see Style). When editing flouts the conventions of classical Hollywood cinema the viewer has to work harder to make sense of a film. This usually impacts on a film's temporal continuity and we can see this in the scene when the Beatles are seen one minute inside the train's compartment and the next standing outside on the tracks. Such ellipses of time are common in art cinema.

The editing style in *A Hard Day's Night* is also influenced by the aesthetic of the French New Wave. Typically, jump cuts and fast, choppy edits reinforce the youthful energy of the film. The editing also helps to establish the occasionally surreal tone of the film, such as when the Beatles switch from playing cards in the luggage compartment of the train to playing their instruments and singing 'I Should Have Known Better'.

Editing can have also have thematic importance. The choice to cut between the scenes of Paul's Grandfather at the casino with the Beatles at the disco gives a clear message about the older generation enjoying a sedate atmosphere in contrast with the young people enjoying themselves in a hot, smoky nightclub. Although the irony is that the young people in this case are behaving themselves whilst the Grandfather is running up a gambling debt.

During the Beatles' performance at the end of the film, the editing works to enhance the sense of real performance, by cutting between the band and the audience, showing images of screaming fans.

contexts

britain at the time of a hard day's night

THE BEATLES AND THE 1960s BABY BOOM

In 1964 the western world was in flux. Twenty years earlier, during the Second World War, millions lost their lives and vast numbers of buildings and cities were decimated. The world was rebuilt anew, and repopulated by the postwar 'baby boom' as families were reunited and relationships begun again.

By 1964 the huge new generation of 'war babies' was approaching adulthood. The result was a furious generational clash, between the established order of adults who had lived through the horror and austerity of the war, and the new youth who had grown up in this fresh, rebuilt world. Change was in the air. Prejudices around race and gender were challenged, and the new youth wanted to rewrite the rulebook.

Throughout the 1950s, American musicians such as Elvis Presley, Carl Perkins and Little Richard had blended together existing musical styles – often from different racial origins – to create rock 'n' roll. This new music was seized on by the world's youth, who perhaps saw in it the vibrancy and cosmopolitan outlook they sought themselves. Teenagers in Liverpool would hear this music from afar on radios with poor reception, or else buy the latest imported singles from America. Amongst these eager fans were the four boys who together formed the Beatles. First known as the Silver Beatles, their name was a conscious pun on that of American rock 'n' roller Buddy Holly's backing band – The Crickets. In turn, the Beatles themselves were the subject of the devotion of the world's youth. The band members found themselves at the forefront of the generational clash of the 1960s. It might be said that they were instrumental in bringing about the acceptance of the ways of the new

experimentation with drugs kept secret

youth. Although they played rock 'n' roll and had unseemly long hair (or so it was seen at the time), their charisma and humour won them the hearts of the older generation, to some degree. They were, perhaps, the band your mother could like too.

Within *A Hard Day's Night*, this intergenerational sparring can be seen almost immediately. Once on board the train to London, the Beatles find themselves sharing a carriage with a cartoonish elderly city gent, in a bowler hat and umbrella. The band verbally spar with the man, and although the tone is good-humoured, there is a steely edge behind the exchanges.

There is a great deal of this generational conflict throughout *A Hard Day's Night* (see Narrative and Form: Themes) and the foremost representative of the older generation is Paul's Grandfather. It's interesting, then, that the Grandfather is revealed to be 'a mixer' – a shady character who actively seeks mischief as soon as his youthful minders let him out of their sight. Undoubtedly this is an ironic reversal of the accepted norm, designed to appeal to the Beatles' obviously pro-youth fans. But in hindsight this sends an intriguing message to viewers – namely, that the accepted order (represented here by the dubious Grandfather) needs to be kept in check by the seemingly anarchic but actually extremely moral younger generation (namely the Beatles).

A Hard Day's Night is very much of its time, capturing that point in their careers when the Beatles represented the acceptable, charming face of the baby boom generation in conflict with the older pre-war order. Later in their career, this conflict moved on to different levels. The Beatles' experimentation with drugs such as marijuana and LSD was kept secret from their elders: at recording sessions, they sneaked away from their own senior **producer**, George Martin, to smoke pot, and famously claimed to have done the same when receiving their MBEs from the Queen at Buckingham Palace. Even their younger fans were left unaware of their drug usage – Paul McCartney's announcement of having smoked marijuana caused uproar in fan publications. The music that resulted from the band's drug experiments – such as 'Strawberry Fields Forever' and the album *Sergeant Pepper's Lonely Hearts Club Band* – even alienated some of their most ardent and open-minded followers. For some, the Beatles' drug experiments were just too much at odds with the norms of 1960s society in Britain. For others – such as the underground 'flower power' or 'hippie' movement – the band were avatars of a fresh new state of mind that would sweep away the old archaic order. This phase of the Beatles' career would come to pass too. In the 1970s, both John Lennon and, to some degree, George Harrison, would continue to dabble in left-field lifestyles or extreme politics. Thirty years later, though, the band members have become respectable elders, albeit forward-thinking ones. Their status is now that befitting middle-aged millionaires, with only occasional forays into music making.

POPULAR CULTURE IN BRITAIN DURING 1964

The world was changing in 1964, and Britain was at the vanguard. British prime minister Harold Wilson promised the 'white heat' of technological revolution under a Labour government, and the cultural life of Britain became rich indeed. The opposing youth groups of the time, the Mods and Rockers, were in pitched battle on the country's seafronts. A third television channel, BBC2, had been launched, whilst BBC1 started a new drama series – the long-running *Doctor Who*. Meanwhile, a satire movement had grown from the stage show *Beyond the Fringe*, centred upon comedian Peter Cook's subsequent opening of a satirical comedy club, *The Establishment*. A satire-based television show, *That Was The Week That Was*, was axed by the BBC for fears of political bias, and literature such as *Fanny Hill* and *Lady Chatterley's Lover* was under scrutiny, facing obscenity charges.

The media was developing into the vast network we know today. 'Swinging London' became accepted as the foremost source of new style in architecture, design and fashion. Meanwhile, the success of the Beatles spawned a host of bands in the North of England, under the banner of 'Merseybeat'. (Notably, *A Hard Day's Night* begins with a literal journey taking the Fab Four to London.) These bands, and their sound, dominated the pop charts in England, and made an impact in America too, where the movement was dubbed 'the British Invasion'. All eyes, it seemed, were on England.

British comedies to take the world's stage

BRITISH CINEMA IN 1964

At the time *A Hard Day's Night* was released, British cinema was also enjoying a boom. The so-called British New Wave featured films including *Room at the Top* (1958), *Saturday Night and Sunday Morning* (1960), *A Taste of Honey* (1961), and *The Loneliness of the Long-Distance Runner* (1962). All of these won international acclaim for their portrayal of modern British life, as well as achieving box office success. These films in turn have their influence on *A Hard Day's Night* (see Style). Less socially relevant, but massively successful in their own right, were the early James Bond films. The series began, on an extremely tight budget, with *Dr No* (1962). An international hit, it was immediately followed by its first sequel, *From Russia With Love* (1963). Although made with American involvement, the James Bond series were essentially British films, made in Britain with a British star. The series continued to dominate the box office throughout the 1960s, and indeed continues still. The Beatles themselves spoofed the series in their second film, *Help!* (1965) (see Contexts: The Beatles' Film Career). In all, the series provided further proof that British cinema was a force to be reckoned with.

The high point of this British film renaissance was *Tom Jones* (1963), an adaptation of Henry Fielding's eighteenth-century novel from *A Taste of Honey* director, Tony Richardson. Shot in full colour, it richly evoked its period setting and its romping style was much admired. It received nine Academy Award nominations, winning four (for direction, score, screenplay adaptation and best picture). The stage was set for further British comedies to take the world's stage, and clearly *A Hard Day's Night* did well to follow in its slipstream.

merchandising

A Hard Day's Night was marketed with a good deal of attendant merchandising, but the question of how much isn't easy to answer. At the time of its release, the Beatles fame had spawned a frenzy of international attention – so-called 'Beatlemania' – and band-related merchandise was produced at a notoriously vast rate. Specific

influence

> powerful and lasting effect on popular culture

influence of a hard day's night

It would have seemed unlikely to United Artists in 1964 that their quickly and cheaply made motion picture – solely devised as an exploitation movie to part Beatles' fans from their money – would have a powerful and lasting effect on popular culture. Nevertheless, the influence of *A Hard Day's Night* continues to be felt to this day.

The concept of a film starring pop musicians certainly wasn't a new idea in 1964. The original pop star, Frank Sinatra, had carved out a substantial parallel career in movies, starring in serious dramas such as *From Here to Eternity* (1953), *The Man With The Golden Arm* (1956) and *The Manchurian Candidate* (1962). Notably, though, Sinatra's career in films was as an actor, and usually a serious one. Only occasionally did Sinatra's film projects involve music, and he never appeared in films as himself. However, his appeal to cinema audiences, at least initially, was not as an actor but as the famous Frank Sinatra, singer.

The Beatles' own inspiration, Elvis Presley, launched a film career with *Love Me Tender* (1956). His acting skills, while hardly exceptional, were deemed to be promising, and music was just a feature of, rather than the focus of, the project. Further films included *Jailhouse Rock* (1957) and *King Creole* (1958), and it seemed as though Presley might carve a good career as a James Dean-style actor. In fact, Presley's entertainment careers were put on hold at the dawn of the 1960s when he was drafted into the US army. Two years later, he was released back into public life, and made over thirty further films. However, the majority of these films were weak, uninspired projects in which Presley portrayed a succession of thinly-disguised versions of himself, which did little to develop his serious acting skills. All these later films also included cheaply made sequences of Presley performing specially-written (and almost uniformly poor) songs. The healthy sales of the soundtrack albums kept the production line for Elvis movies in motion, but in overview his acting career was an embarrassment – a disappointment at best.

merchandise was sold, but the film is, of course, Beatles merchandising of itself. Ironically, the film deal was struck with United Artists purely for the intention of producing a lucrative soundtrack. Not only is the film itself a piece of merchandising; it was actually made because of merchandising.

Dedicated *A Hard Day's Night* merchandise included a novelisation by John Burke, including eight pages of stills from the film, which sold well. The crucial soundtrack as well was enormously successful; advance sales alone (which stood at over two million copies) put the film in profit before its actual release. At the time, it was the best-selling album ever. Different versions were, however, released in different markets. The UK album featured the eight songs recorded for the film (including 'You Can't Do That', which was dropped from the film itself) plus five songs recorded in June 1964, after the film was completed.

The US version dropped 'You Can't Do That' and four of the five new songs, which were held over for later releases. Instead it features four instrumental versions of Beatles songs, as performed for the film by the George Martin Orchestra. To George Martin's pride, his track 'Ringo Theme' (an instrumental of the Beatles' earlier song 'This Boy', which plays in the film as Ringo goes out 'parading') received considerable airplay of its own on radio stations in America.

The poster for the film has become a design classic. In keeping with the film's documentary overtones, the poster features four sets of photographic 'contact sheets' of the band members, each image showing a portrait of a Beatle in a different pose or expression. The poster indicates that the film will show the Beatles in close-up, intimately displaying a whole range of emotions.

The film itself may not live up to this, but the poster image has been enshrined as a classic of sixties design, comparable perhaps to Warhol's prints of Marilyn Monroe, featuring as they do a grid of photographic images of popular icons.

a careful blend of verve and imagination

England's foremost answer to Elvis was Cliff Richard. Along with his backing band, 'The Shadows', Cliff appeared in a number of song-based British films including *Expresso Bongo* (1959), *The Young Ones* (1961) and *Summer Holiday* (1962). Although reasonable fare, Cliff's film career is on a par with Elvis's. Another influential British 'rocker', Tommy Steele, starred in films such as *The Tommy Steele Story* (1957) and *The Duke Wore Jeans* (1958).

Certainly the history of the pop-star vehicle as it stood did not augur well for the Beatles' film. *A Hard Day's Night* succeeds, however, through a careful blend of verve and imagination. Quite simply, the finished film captures and communicates the magic of the Beatles' music and performance, in the form of cinema. This is how it succeeds where previous pop movies had failed – or else had not had the skill to try. The film isn't simply the opening of a new brand of show business for its stars to mine: it is an organic extension of the band themselves.

The success of *A Hard Day's Night,* with both the public and critics, led to its influence impacting on other films. Amongst others, the Beatles-inspired Dave Clark Five starred in their own swinging sixties feature *Catch Us If You Can* (1966). Merseybeat band Gerry and the Pacemakers made their only film outing (alongside Cilla Black) in the Liverpool-set *Ferry Cross the Mersey* (1964), as themselves as a struggling band.

Naturally, the success of the Beatles' film also went a long way towards shaping its sequel. Richard Lester was engaged to direct the follow-up, and many elements of the first film were repeated (see Contexts: The Beatles Film Career). This time, though, the Beatles would appear in full colour. The documentary touches of *A Hard Day's Night* were abandoned, and the result is a more cartoonish, almost surreal experience. Whereas the band were a solid gang unit in their first film, in *Help!* (1965) they actually share a bizarre extended house. The proposed third Beatles film was a troubled project and the Beatles film formula was not to be used again or developed. As such *A Hard Day's Night* and *Help!* stand in many ways as one unit – that of the Beatles' live-action film adventures.

Nowhere was the influence of the films more keenly felt than in the television series *The Monkees* (1966-7). Made by Columbia's television massive impact on public perception

division Screen Gems, the blatant reasoning behind the series was to ape the Beatles' film success. In this case, a group of four actors and musicians was manufactured specifically, and appeared in mad-cap adventures about the band. Like the Beatles, they shared a house and went under their own names. Each television episode featured two song sequences, in which the action would stop – or else mutate into, for instance, a chase scene – as the band performed. The songs, released on spin-off soundtrack albums, were mainly written and played by musicians other than the real Monkees. Even the Beatles declared themselves to be fans of the series. In a peculiar twist, The Monkees themselves rebelled against their record company bosses, and began to write and perform their own music as of their third album. They even made a feature film, *Head* (1968), which helped finish their career. Now appreciated as an imaginative and intelligent work, it bears little of the hallmarks of the Beatles' own films which had inspired The Monkees creation just two years earlier.

The influence of *A Hard Day's Night* is far reaching. Crucially, it had a massive and often underestimated impact on the public perception of the Beatles themselves. Before the film's release, the band had experienced snowballing chart success, but as personalities they were little exposed. They were regular guests on the BBC radio series 'Saturday Club', on which they exchanged banter with host Bernie Matthews between songs. Something of this good-humoured charm was extended to a series of Christmas flexi-discs exclusive to members of the band's fan club: the first was recorded for Christmas 1963. Mainly, though, the band would only be known to their fans through radio appearances and occasional press conference footage shown in cinemas as part of the Pathe newsreels that would accompany feature film screenings. As regards attendance of a live Beatles performance, the onset of 'Beatlemania' and its attendant deafening screams from female fans would ensure that little of the band's individual personalities would come across.

The script for *A Hard Day's Night* was carefully tailored to the band members, and writer Alun Owen spent some time with the band to

'a turning point in my life'

research them as individuals before embarking on the job of writing their lines. This approach had limited worth according to the band themselves (see Background: Making *A Hard Day's Night*).

Nevertheless, the Beatles as they appeared in *A Hard Day's Night* were familiar enough as the personalities who quipped amongst themselves in their public appearances, and the film intentionally bore the patina of a documentary insight into their lives. This was always the intention behind the film – that it be sold to Beatles fans as a true window into the real band.

As a result, the perhaps simplistic personalities given to John, Paul, Ringo and George within the film stuck with the public at large. Their public personae were to some degree forged by Alun Owen and Richard Lester. In *A Hard Day's Night* the Beatles were on show. When, several years later, admissions of drug-taking and adultery were made by the beloved band members, their fans were in uproar. Indeed, it's hard to believe the good-hearted rascals from *A Hard Day's Night* could be capable of worse than tomfoolery. All subsequent Beatles films portray the band members in much the same mould as in their first film (see Contexts: Beatles' Film Career). However, it's debatable to what degree this is because they truly were as they were shown to be in *A Hard Day's Night*, and to what degree the four caricatures from that film have simply stuck. Either way, *A Hard Day's Night* set the Beatles' characters in stone in the public eye.

Still, the Beatles' appearance in the film was an inspiration in itself. Across the Atlantic, fans of the British invasion were galvanised into action by the film: the four members of the Byrds were entranced by it, as one of them – David Crosby – explains: '*A Hard Day's Night* was a turning point in my life. We [the Byrds] went to see it together ... I came out and swung around a post at arm's length going "Yes!". I went into that movie and came out knowing what I wanted to do with the rest of my life' (Carr, 1997, p. 27).

The film also created a template for all subsequent pop bands, should they attempt to break into the field of cinema. In the 1970s, glam stompers Slade attempted to make the leap, with *Flame* (1973). The members of Slade here double as the fictional band *Flame*, whose rise

Spiceworld has similarities to *A Hard Day's Night*

and fall the film details. Although ostensibly a dark, cynical tale of talented young hopefuls tangling with the machinations of a brutal music industry, Flame nevertheless follows in the footsteps of *A Hard Day's Night*. Here, though, the documentary feel is taken to greater extremes. Sequences of gang-style interband humour, and the song sequences, reveal the debt to the Beatles' debut.

More recently, the self-styled 'Fab Five', the Spice Girls, made an abortive leap to feature film with *Spiceworld* (1997). With over thirty years' distance, it was entirely reasonable for this venture to wear on its sleeve its intention to be *A Hard Day's Night* for the 1990s. Following the often unlikely tribulations of the Spice Girls in the run up to a massive and important gig, *Spiceworld* features a cavalcade of British celebrity cameos and a slew of opportunities for the band themselves to display and endorse 'girl power'.

Tellingly, *Spiceworld* has only basic similarities to *A Hard Day's Night*. In fact, any pop musician's film vehicle can be said to owe a good deal to *A Hard Day's Night*, whatever its tone or structure. This is simply because *A Hard Day's Night* was groundbreaking in its attempts to use pop celebrities and their music within cinema, whilst aping their public personae rather than forcing them to play an unlikely acting role. *A Hard Day's Night* is an extension of, rather than a divergence from, its stars' music and personalities. It is this extension that is groundbreaking about the film: it is pop cinema. All subsequent entries in the genre follow in its slipstream.

This technique was further refined in *Help!* (1965) the following year: the stand-out sequence in the latter film accompanying 'Ticket to Ride' – a similar outdoor free-for-all as the band ski on the Austrian Alps (and, briefly, appear to mime to the song with a piano). In this way, *A Hard Day's Night* predates the notional 'first music video' – that made for rock group Queen's 'Bohemian Rhapsody' in 1975 – by eleven years.

Clearly, though, the look and feel of, in particular, the 'Can't Buy Me Love' sequence, lays the ground for the music video and subsequently for MTV. (Ironically, the MTV format was actually put together by music video

shorthand for sixties-inspired popular culture

pioneer Mike Nesmith – formerly a member of The Monkees and hence a disciple of the Richard Lester Beatles' films.) According to Lester, he was once sent a vellum scroll which proclaimed him to be 'the father of MTV'. The director dryly replied that he wanted a blood test. The director now declares, 'I don't think one ever sits down and says, "I'm going to do something at this point which ... will be known in ten year's time as MTV"' ... you don't do it for those reasons, you do it because you think "what do you need at this point?"'.

The portrayal of the Beatles in *A Hard Day's Night* set their public personas in stone. As the film itself is so crucial to the band's career, it's unsurprising that ex-Monty Python comedian Eric Idle uses the film comprehensively in his Beatles spoof, *The Rutles: All You Need Is Cash* (1978). The Rutles are a comic approximation of the Beatles, named in honour of Idle's television series 'Rutland Weekend Television'. Many of the fictional band's songs ape Beatles originals: 'A Hard Day's Night' becomes 'A Hard Day's Rut', with an eponymous film featured within the spoof. The famed poster of *A Hard Day's Night* is also used to feature portraits of Rutles members, with the resulting version also serving as the film spoof's own poster.

A Hard Day's Night itself continues to be referenced as a pop culture artefact. The opening of *Austin Powers: International Man of Mystery* (1997) shows the eponymous celebrity spy trying to flee and hide from his pursuing female fans. With its cartoon representation of Swinging Sixties London, the sequence amounts to a full-colour spoof of the opening chase from the Beatles' debut.

High Fidelity (2000) tells the story of Rob, a record shop owner and pop music obsessive; the film's poster clearly apes that of *A Hard Day's Night*, showing as it does a similar array of lop-sided portraits of the film's star, John Cusack. Almost forty years old, *A Hard Day's Night* stands as the quintessential pop music film, and referencing the film has become a shorthand for sixties-inspired popular culture.

changed the face of popular music

the beatles' film career

United Artists' contract with the Beatles was for a total of three feature films. After the runaway success of *A Hard Day's Night*, the search was on for the projects that could form the next two films.

The project code-named *Beatles 2* was relatively straightforward to make. Richard Lester was again signed up as director. An early plan was to show Ringo cursing the relentless claustrophobia of a pop star's life, and drunkenly engaging a nearby hitman to end his misery. The ensuing movie would feature a now all-too-sober Ringo fleeing with the rest of the band, with the eager hit-man in hot pursuit.

This story was abandoned, although it mirrors the resultant *Help!* (1965) in many ways. Ringo – having been judged to be the strongest actor amongst the band – is showcased here, as he unwittingly becomes the owner of the sacrificial ring of the cult of the goddess Kaili, and the Beatles are pursued across England, the Austrian Alps and the sunny Bahamas by acolytes of Kaili, desperate to recover the ring.

The quest for the title was easier the second time around. Although initially heralded as *Eight Arms To Hold You*, Lester quickly settled on *Help!* and the Beatles had written and recorded the title song within thirty hours of the decision. By 1966, the Beatles had announced the end of their career as a touring band, and concentrated instead on experimenting with the sound and production of their records. The albums that followed – including *Revolver, Sergeant Pepper's Lonely Hearts Club Band* and the so-called *White Album* – changed the face of popular music. Meanwhile, the quest for the proposed *Beatles 3* dragged on. Various projects came to nothing. Advanced plans were in place to adapt Richard Condon's novel *A Talent For Loving* for the band – which would be set in 1871 and feature them as pioneers in the American West taking part in a cross-country horse race from the Rio Grande. This project collapsed, as did later plans to film both *The Three Musketeers* and *The Lord of the Rings* as vehicles for the Beatles. (The luminary likes of both David Lean and Stanley Kubrick were seriously approached with a view to directing the latter.)

Another proposal was a film wherein the four Beatles would appear as different aspects of the same character, suffering from a split personality. A script, entitled *Shades of a Personality*, was written, and Michelangelo Antonioni, the director of the acclaimed 'swinging London' film *Blow Up* (1966), was in the frame as a director. Although plans were advanced, and filming was due to take place in Spain in early 1967, this project was shelved too.

Soon after, the script was totally reworked by controversial Leicester-born playwright Joe Orton, the author of the plays *Entertaining Mr Sloane* and *Loot*. The result was *Up Against It*, an extremely provocative script in which the central characters are outlaws in a fictional foreign state. As Orton confided to his infamous diary, 'in my script they have been caught in flagrante, become involved in dubious political activity, dressed as women, committed murder, been put in prison and committed adultery'. Unsurprisingly, the script was rejected by Walter Shenson. In the event, Richard Lester elected to film it without the Beatles – but this avenue too was closed when Orton was suddenly, brutally murdered by his embittered boyfriend.

Between 1967 and 1970, three Beatles films were actually released. The first, *Magical Mystery Tour* (1967), was a TV film directed, written and edited by the band themselves. Although conceived by Paul McCartney as a scheme to occupy the rudderless band after the unexpected death of their legendary manager, Brian Epstein, the end result suffered from a lack of firm authority. Although nowadays regarded as an admittedly disjointed but unusual and charming piece, the film resulted from the band hiring a bus, painting it in psychedelic hues and driving it around the English countryside with a group of hand-picked eccentrics as passengers, and was relentlessly slated on transmission.

In 1968, *Yellow Submarine* was released. This fully animated feature, based around a number of classic Beatles songs and a handful of their 'cast-offs', was an offshoot of the Beatles cartoon – an anodyne television series made by King Features of America. The series had showcased crude animations, unconvincing approximations of the Beatles' voices and rather basic storylines. The band themselves had

changed the face of popular music

accordingly low expectations of the film equivalent, but in fact the lavish animations of director George Dunning and his team make for a visual feast. In many ways, *Yellow Submarine* is the psychedelic romp that *Magical Mystery Tour* fell short of being. A vast range of merchandise spun off from the film, and it was re-released to much acclaim in 1999.

As it was released through United Artists, the Beatles had assumed that *Yellow Submarine* counted as the third and last film in their contract for the company. However, as the film was animated, and didn't actually feature the band in person (except for a brief cameo), it didn't count towards fulfilling the original contract. *Beatles 3* still remained to be made. It eventually arrived in 1970, in the form of *Let It Be*. Originally, filming had taken place in early 1969 for what was then planned to be a television film. First known as *Get Back*, the idea had been to film the band at work on their latest album, one which would be recorded live and without studio trickery – hence 'getting back' to basics.

These filmed sessions had demonstrated much tension within the band, as the four members began irrevocably to split apart. The film and accompanying soundtrack album were both shelved as the Beatles instead recorded their intended farewell album, 'Abbey Road'. The footage was eventually edited together by director Michael Lindsay-Hogg and given a full theatrical release as *Let It Be* in 1970, thereby fulfilling the third and final part of the Beatles' United Artists contract, and hence their film career.

conclusion

A Hard Day's Night achieves the extremely unlikely. It takes a thin format, and with little time or money the film's makers created something remarkable: something which documents and comments on the predicament of its real-life stars. Intended as a quick pop movie, the result changed the face of the genre completely, and its influence is clearly felt throughout popular culture to this day.

bibliography

general film

Altman, Rick, *Film Genre*, BFI, 1999
Detailed exploration of the concept of film genre

Bordwell, David, *Narration in the Fiction Film*, Routledge, 1985
A detailed study of narrative theory and structures

– – –, Staiger, Janet & Thompson, Kristin, *The Classical Hollywood Cinema: Film Style & Mode of Production to 1960*, Routledge, 1985; pbk 1995
An authoritative study of cinema as institution, it covers film style and production

– – – & Thompson, Kristin, *Film Art*, McGraw-Hill, 4th edn, 1993
An introduction to film aesthetics for the non-specialist

Branson, Gill & Stafford, Roy, *The Media Student's Handbook*, Routledge, 2nd edn, 1999

Buckland, Warren, *Teach Yourself Film Studies*, Hodder & Stoughton, 1998
Very accessible, it gives an overview of key areas in film studies

Cook, Pam & Bernink, Mieke (eds), *The Cinema Book*, BFI, 2nd edn, 1999

Corrigan, Tim, *A Short Guide To Writing About Film*, HarperCollins, 1994
What it says: a practical guide for students

Dyer, Richard (with Paul McDonald), *Stars*, BFI, 2nd edn, 1998
A good introduction to the star system

Easthope, Antony, *Classical Film Theory*, Longman, 1993
A clear overview of writing about film theory

Hayward, Susan, *Key Concepts in Cinema Studies*, Routledge, 1996

Hill, John & Gibson, Pamela Church (eds), *The Oxford Guide to Film Studies*, Oxford University Press, 1998
Wide-ranging standard guide

Lapsley, Robert & Westlake, Michael, *Film Theory: An Introduction*, Manchester University Press, 1994

Maltby, Richard & Craven, Ian, *Hollywood Cinema*, Blackwell, 1995
A comprehensive work on the Hollywood industry and its products

Mulvey, Laura, 'Visual Pleasure and Narrative Cinema' (1974), in *Visual and Other Pleasures*, Indiana University Press, Bloomington, 1989
The classic analysis of 'the look' and 'the male gaze' in Hollywood cinema. Also available in numerous other edited collections

Nelmes, Jill (ed.), *Introduction to Film Studies*, Routledge, 2nd edn, 1999
Deals with several national cinemas and key concepts in film study

Nowell-Smith, Geoffrey (ed.), *The Oxford History of World Cinema*, Oxford University Press, 1996
Hugely detailed and wide-ranging with many features on 'stars'

Thomson, David, *A Biographical Dictionary of the Cinema*, Secker & Warburg, 1975
  Unashamedly driven by personal taste, but often stimulating

Truffaut, François, *Hitchcock*, Simon & Schuster, 1966, rev. edn. Touchstone, 1985
  Landmark extended interview

Turner, Graeme, *Film as Social Practice*, 3rd edn, Routledge, 1999
  Chapter four, 'Film Narrative', discusses structuralist theories of narrative

Wollen, Peter, *Signs and Meaning in the Cinema*, BFI 1997 (revised edn)
  An important study in semiology

Readers should also explore the many relevant websites and journals. *Film Education* and *Sight and Sound* are standard reading.

Valuable websites include:

The Internet Movie Database at www.uk.imdb.com

Screensite at www.tcf.ua.edu/screensite/contents.html

The Media and Communications Site at the University of Aberystwyth at www.aber.ac.uk/~dgc/welcome.html

There are obviously many other university and studio websites which are worth exploring in relation to film studies.

a hard day's night

Carr, Roy, *The Beatles at the Movies*, UFO Music, 1996

MacDonald, Ian, *Revolution in the Head*, Pimlico, 1994

Neaverson, Bob, *The Beatles Movies*, Cassell, 1997

Norman, Philip, *Shout!*, Corgi, 1981

Walker, Alexander, *Hollywood England*, Harrap, 1974

***The Beatles Anthology*,** The Beatles, Cassell, 2000

***You Can't Do That!*,** VCI Video, 1994

***Richard Lester NFT Interview*,** BFI, 1999

cinematic terms

antagonist the main character's opponent: the film's villain. If the protagonist is said to be on some kind of 'quest', the antagonist is the character placing obstacles in his path

auteur literally the 'author' of the film. An auteur has a strong individual style and favoured themes, and is the chief creative force within the film. A director of note may be tagged 'auteur', implying their vision is paramount. Occasionally, a strong screenwriter or even actor, might be called an 'auteur'

cinematography the basic term for 'cinema photography' – any treatment of the physical film image, be it during filming or during laboratory developing

cinematographer essentially the role liaising between the director and the camera operators. Responsible for translating the director's conception of shots into actual camerawork. Noted cinematographers can have an impact of the look of a film on screen equal to – or even greater than – the director's

closure a film's narrative can be said to have reached full closure when all strands of the narrative have been tied up at the conclusion. Alternatively, events may have been set into motion that haven't been seen through to their conclusion, and closure is thereby only partial

cut the immediate linking of two shots within a film

diegesis all elements within the world of the frame, including characters, props and sound

director the individual responsible for overseeing the shooting – deciding which shots to film, and liaising with cast and crew. The importance of the role can change – 'second unit' directors might shoot secondary scenes, and the director need not always be involved in editing – but the director is ultimately in charge of getting the screenplay on film

editing the post-production of joining together selected shots by cuts, fades or wipes, to create the seamless flow of the film's narrative. A good deal of a film's ultimate effect can be created through well-judged editing, and a director will therefore usually be closely involved

exploitation picture a film designed solely to make money, by 'exploiting' a demand for a particular genre or gimmick

frame the shaped image on screen, making use of objects and actors, most often composed by the director

genre a type of film identifiable by recurrent use of conventions – such as science-fiction, horror or action films

lens the clear opening into a film camera, and therefore the 'eye' through which the viewer sees the finished film. Lenses differ, and a specific lens effect can alter the texture of a film. For example, telephoto lenses create a flat, two-dimensional image, whereas wide-angled lenses give three-dimensional depth of field

mise-en-scène the chosen contents of the frame, from sets and props to actors and special effects

motif any element that recurs in a film to cumulative effect, relating to a theme. It may be sound, an image or a setting. By way of example, *Don't Look Now* (1973) makes repeated use of the colour red, and of water

cinematic terms

plot the sequence of events shown within a film. This need not follow the chronological story

producer responding for creating and setting up a film production. Whereas the director oversees the hands-on filming, the producer takes charge of more executive, often financial matters pertaining to a film, and usually has less of a creative role

protagonist the main character in the film. Most stories can be seen as some kind of quest. The protagonist is therefore the character whose quest the film depicts

screenplay the initial script of the film, featuring directions, descriptions and dialogue, laid out to a set format. May differ from the finished film should changes be made during shooting

shot a single image – be it mobile or static – within a film, completed by a cut. Certain standard shot sizes are best described in terms of how a human figure is framed: **long shot** – a full standing figure; **medium close-up** – head to chest of a figure; **close-up** – head, and perhaps shoulders, of a figure; **extreme** (or **big**) **close-up** – the face only, or a single expression

space the physical space between objects in a shot. Space could only be given proper consideration once lenses became available that could lend three-dimensional depth of field to a shot, by allowing objects in the background to be in sharp focus, at the same time as the foreground. Hence in *Citizen Kane* (1947), characters moving from the foreground to the background of a shot represents their lessened importance

stereotype an oversimplified, one-dimensional character, identifiable by certain characteristics – such as a 'mousy housewife' or a 'brash American'. Most often either a deliberate target for ridicule, or else the result of poorly developed writing or acting

story the chronological sequence of events touched on within a film. However, the film follows a plot, and the sequence may be altered, or events simply not shown

take a single, uninterrupted run of film in a camera. Several takes may be made of a single scene, and one take selected to form the actual shot in the finished film

A HARD DAY'S NIGHT

credits

production company
United Artists

director
Richard Lester

producer
Walter Shenson

screenplay
Alun Owen

cinematographer
Gilbert Taylor

editor
John Jympson

music director
George Martin

costumes
Julia Harris

art director
Ray Simm

cast
The Beatles – Themselves

Wilfred Brambell – Grandfather

Norman Rossington – Norm

John Junkin – Shake

Victor Spinetti – TV Director

Kenneth Haigh –
Advertising Executive

Anna Quayle – Millie

Deryck Guyler – Police Sergeant

songs
The Beatles, Can't Buy Me Love

The Beatles,
I Should Have Known Better

The Beatles, If I Fell

The Beatles, I'm Happy Just to
Dance With You

The Beatles, And I Love Her

The Beatles, Tell Me Why